Life Door

*Feed your mind, body and soul your
unfinished business*

NANCY LYNN MARTIN

iUniverse, Inc.
New York   Bloomington

iUniverse books may be ordered through booksellers or by contacting:

iUniverse
1663 Liberty Drive
Bloomington, IN 47403
www.iuniverse.com
1-800-Authors (1-800-288-4677)

Because of the dynamic nature of the Internet, any Web addresses or links contained in this book may have changed since publication and may no longer be valid. The views expressed in this work are solely those of the author and do not necessarily reflect the views of the publisher, and the publisher hereby disclaims any responsibility for them.

ISBN: 978-1-4401-7823-8 (sc)
ISBN: 978-1-4401-7824-5 (ebook)

Printed in the United States of America

iUniverse rev. date: 12/5/2009

In memory of my Grandma Veetmeier

I deeply appreciate your presence that is in my life. I know you are with me always just as you taught me that God is with me always. I thank you for your ever present unconditional love along with God. You are my inspiration- always have been- always will be. When I read my Daily Words now, I feel you are reading them with me, praying to God. Every time I hear your favorite piano selections I think of you. I have your blue cross made of crochet up in my kitchen wall along with your dancing photos. I love you. Love, Your Nancy

In memory of Danny my son

I am grateful for all the blessings bestowed on me so far, you along with Jenny and Jake being the greatest blessings of all. I am aware that I need to always live in the present moment and embrace those moments with the utmost care. Your short 10 years taught me so much. I was the student and you were the teacher. I know now that you fulfilled your assignment and that God sometimes brings His creations home early. Thank you for giving us the gift of your presence. I love you. Love Mom

Contents

Acknowledgments And Gratitude

I am grateful first and foremost for my daughter Jenny and son Jake. Raising you has been my utmost happiness. Your idiosyncrasies and your joyful silliness and individualities are truly a source of joy for me. Thank you for the gift of your presence and your everlasting loving ways. You are true blessings to me. All memories are near and dear to me and I look forward to many more. Thank you for encouragement.

As far as you are concerned, Jenny (my daughter) Thank you for your help with this book. Thank you also for nursing me through my recovery the last couple of months. Thank you for all our talks.

Thank you, Jake (my son) for all your help with this book including the book cover design. Thank you for giving me the books, The Pilgrimage, Way of the Peaceful Warrior, and Treasury of Women's Quotations. Thank you for all our talks.

I love you both Jenny and Jake. Love Mom

Thank you to all that have been in my life so far whether it is for a reason, season, or lifetime. Every one of you are true blessings to me including those who have been challenges to me. I hold all memories near and dear to me. All of you were in my life for a reason. All have been my mentors along with God and the universe.

May all of you have the life you search for.
Peace to all of you

LIFE DOOR
FEED YOUR MIND BODY AND SOUL
YOUR UNFINISHED BUSINESS

Preface

Only the universe knows the final outcome of everything. We chart our course but must always leave room for the unexpected from the universe. We need to be able to be flexible with advice from others and for surprises in life or we will be truly disappointed.

There is nothing wrong with listening to other peoples stories, in fact I encourage it. I myself wouldn't be writing a self help book if I didn't think that we all are teachers and students and that it is our purpose here on earth to serve one another. Others can lead but you have to make it happen. You receive the ball, now what do you intend to do with it? This is the part that is up to you. Your thoughts, feelings, free will, choices and divine order need to be a part of your individual progress to a situation. We actually have to go through the process ourself. The term "God willing" (or actually your will and action on that will) is part of the process of where your journey will take you. The universe hears all of our prayers but sometimes the answer is no and your prayer will be answered in a different way other than what you expect. It may not be the right time and maybe something is being prepared for you that will be best for all those concerned.

We are to take into consideration what others are communicating to us and apply our own experiences. When you go *through* experiences and not *around* them you will begin to have the "ah -ha" moments and then and only then will you appreciate the writings and advice of others. You will also find spirituality and be flexible to the universes unexpected events. The common denominator must always be individual awakening to something.

Have you ever read a book and said to yourself "Yeah well, that's easy for them to say. They didn't have the childhood I had or they don't have the nasty boss I have to deal with." How many books do you have laying around with your mental image staring at you saying "That's them not me?" Take care of your unfinished business and change your attitude. This is the time to clean your attic (your mind). We all need to clear baggage in order to grow and get on with the life we were sent here to live. We need love and peace in the world and omit violence and war. That's the goal.

There are many doors in life. What you do with the doors is always your choice. Here's my comparison of the doors and the glass theory. Is your glass 1\2 full or 1\2 empty? I say it depends on what you have in the glass. If you are working on adding positivity, than you want it 1\2 full. This is showing that you are making progress filling it to the brim or even letting your cup runnith over. If you are working on voiding out negativity, than you want the glass 1\2 empty because it's showing that you are making progress to eliminate it and are working to empty it.

You can ask yourself the same questions about the doors. Do you keep the doors of your life closed, open, 1\2 closed, 1\2 open? Do you find opportunity behind a door and not go with the flow because you *think* you can't do something, or do you go with the flow with all the gusto you have? Again these are all choices *you* have.

If you can't relate to *my* door of opportunity in your life, than replace the doors and windows of your soul with something that relates more to you as an individual. Maybe you like to cook. Think in terms of all the ingredients you use as being experiences. Create new "dishes" with existing ones and replace what you no longer care for. Replace an ingredient with another. Did your choice make the dish taste different? You always have a choice. Changes take place when you are willing to make the change and than actually acting on that will. You will be surprised at the outcome. If things aren't working in your life, than try something different.

Don't get into the someday, shoulda, woulda, coulda mode. These will always lead to disappointment and regrets. These always lead to some type of an addiction rut that will prove to be a nightmare in the long run.

We all can relate to computers. Become a computer. Reprogram your thoughts to serve you in positive ways. When you find negativity in your life that is not serving you spiritually, first find the positive to it, than learn from it, than all you have to do is click the delete button. You can also store it for awhile in case you have to re-learn it.

Maybe water sports or fishing is your thing. We all need to be skimmers and swimmers in this big sea of life. Skim off the best parts that will benefit all those concerned and then swim by propelling yourself through the sea of life in a smoother way. Reading about others experiences are to help change our direction if need be, but we have to do our own swimming. When your life goes off it's charted course for what ever reasons, you need to know what toxic fish to let go and which ones to keep to serve your body well. Don't just wait for your ship to come in, help put the winds in your sails and don't ever let anyone take the winds out of your sails.

How about gardening and all those pesky weeds or bugs eating away at your flowers, fruits and veges. You know first hand that some of these pests are actually beneficial. You learn about the choices you have and take great care to see what works and what doesn't. Apply this same theory to your life.

You can apply just about anything you want to all parts of this book. Just relate what I write to something that will serve you and others. If you really dig deep into the open doors of your soul, the mixing bowl, your computer warehouse mind, the sea, your garden or whatever, you surly will find your own power.

After each chapter I have a journal section for you to write your thoughts and feelings in. This is where you can weed out/delete what will not serve you and replace what will serve you in your individual life. What works for one may not work for another.

Read, experience, be aware and beware, be flexible, apply your own individuality, journal your feelings and thoughts during the process, listen to your soul power, and invite the unexpected that will provide you with new found strength and awaken your spirituality.

(Book ref 0): *"Language of Letting Go"* by Melody Beattie, she says in Step 12 "We do our own recovery work and become a living demonstration of hope, self love, comfort, and health."

I believe that the 12 Steps of Alcoholic Anonymous should be worked through in all of our lives. We all have an addiction to something and the sooner we are honest about that, the sooner we can all get through the steps of recovery (any type of recovery). One by one we can make a better world for all to live in.

Brief summary of the 12 Steps:

1. Admit to the situation at hand
2. Believe in higher power
3. Surrender
4. Take inventory of self
5. Be honest
6. Let go of that which is no longer useful
7. Let go of old feelings/beliefs
8. Heal by putting feelings in journal
9. Take responsibility
10. Stay on track, focus, be aware
11. Pray for strength, not gimme gimme
12. Receive spiritual awakening because you went through all the recovery steps

Remember addictions can be anything. Addicted to food, shopping, worry, hoarding, people, phobias, obsessed with ideas or beliefs, and the list goes on and on. Everyone is addicted to something and that is the major cause of being stuck somewhere in our life and not being able to move on.

Introduction

My intention of this book/journal is to hopefully lead you to a more joyous journey. We all have our own lessons to learn through tests, messages, and obstacles so that we can grow. We would be doing our mind, body and soul a great deal of good if we would make an adventure of our journey by finding pleasures along the path. We need to invite tests, messages, and obstacles to be our friends. We need to connect mind, body and soul in every waking hour and embrace them like there is no tomorrow, because we are all not guaranteed tomorrow.

(Quote ref. 1) by Robert Browning *"What are we on this earth for if it is not to grow."*

(Daily Word ref. 1) "I am receptive to new ideas and greater possibilities for growth."

(Quote ref. 2) by Gail Sheehy *"If we don't change, we don't grow. If we don't grow, we aren't really living."*

I've added blank journal pages for you to write feelings and jot down progress towards growth. If I write something that doesn't make sense to you, than add what makes sense to you and find quotations and affirmations that make sense to you. This book/journal is intended for everyone 13 years old to 100+ young.

(Book ref. 1) According to Venice Bloodworth in her book *"Key to Yourself"* "It doesn't matter how many years you have lived. You are only 11 months old now. Your body is constantly being renewed." She also says "Thinking is the true business of life." She calls this the "Thought law".

Formulas

When you were in (or now in) school, you studied history, math, science, language arts, etc. Most subjects had so called concrete *formulas* for you to follow. History, however, has time lines that were charted through the ages. These could just be beliefs, altered opinions or the way someone perceived something. This falls into the 3 fold law - The way I saw it, the way you saw it, and the way it really was. I call formulas "Givens" for solutions, or "We give in" to something because thats the way to do it, or so we're told.

When you are around 13, you realize that there is no formula for life. You're saying (show me the *DOOR* to the class about *LIFE*) but there is none. You get all different opinions, answers, options, and sometimes outrageous comments based on what people think. You are confused, scared, and alone and want to tell and sometimes do tell everyone to go to (H-E double hockey sticks.) We are taught formulas (comfort zones). They are safe rules for doing something. Formulas are of some good but they do not leave room for *growth* or *change*. They don't work in life because we can never know the *true* outcome of something. What works for some will not work for others. There is, however, a common thread and it's called the universe.

The universe always has the final say! The words trials and tribulations are shun by many. I like to use the word *experiences*. Experiences are what you need to go through, but you can't apply a tried and true formula to them because we all have different experiences according to our *assignments* in life. We also have *choices* and *free will*, hence again, no formula can be applied. Then of course we have the divine plan that always surprises us with the unexpected.

(Quote ref. 3) by Ralph Waldo Emerson *"Life is a series of surprises."*

Get ready for the ride (of) your life and (for) your life! Enjoy your journey. Let the dance continue and enjoy the ride.

PART ONE

Part One

Chapter 1

Buddies With The Universe

So, if the universe has the final say, doesn't it stand to reason that we need to be buddies with the universe? If you need a formula to life, that's it, but it will not be given to you. You need to go through (not around) tests. You need to pursue why you are here. Your assignment is to find your assignment that will serve yourself and others.

(Quote ref. 4) by Sir Wilfred Grenfell *"The service we render others is really the rent we pay for our room on earth."*

Once you find out your assignment (your creative talent) you will fall into work that you love and can then spread love to others and serve others. This is the way to bring you joy, but you need to pursue it.

(Quote ref. 5) by Unknown *"Happiness has no recipe, each person must cook it with the flavor of their own meditations."*

Sometimes you are in jobs or situations that you don't really like. See this as a stepping stone to reach your real assignment/purpose. You will be surprised how those jobs connect to your real assignment (or better yet) form your own individual unique character. Learn all you can and apply it to your life. Nothing is by accident, there is always a reason. Be aware of all tests that are being presented to you. Ask, what is this now? Seek, the answer. Knock, and say how can I use this experience for the greater good of all those concerned? You will know when to move on. Find talent, serve with it, spread love, make money…a living and a life.

(Quote ref. 6) by John Dewey, American philosopher and educational reformer: *"To find out what one is fitted to do, and to secure an opportunity to do it, is the key to happiness."*

In most cases I use the word universe but everyone also needs to look to their own *soul power* spiritual coach. I personally have been an avid reader of *"Daily Word"* (Silent Unity.) In this book I quote the Bible, quotations, lyrics, books, and Daily Word. Worship is very personal and everyone needs to connect with their "soul power" spiritual coach each and every day.

Chapter 2

Spirituality
You Must Break First In Order To Heal

You find your spirituality by finding the connection of mind, body and soul. Spirituality is the universal window both individually and globally. It generates kindness, love, understanding, peace and integrity. It is a partnership with God or whoever your "soul power" is. Doesn't matter what religion doctrine you believe in. We are all united. The meditating Buddha for example is a symbol of love, peace and serves others, the same as Jesus. This is spirituality unity because it gives you deep feelings and unique experiences. Religion divides us because of traditional dogma and rigid rules. When you are spiritually awakened, you know that you can break the chains that bind you. You gain faith that you can change behaviors and habits which will in turn bring good to yourself and all others concerned. You learn to hang in and persevere even the tough times because that is when your opportunities for growth will either make you or break you. Actually you will break first in order to become whole and heal.

(Quote ref. 7) by Frederick the Great *"All religions must be tolerated, for every man must go to heaven in his own way."*

Everyone has the right to believe in something, but if you find yourself losing yourself in any way, shape, or form, because of a belief, than I would suggest charting a different course for yourself. Remember that your soul is not for sale. Sometimes you lose yourself, however, in order to figure something out. Sometimes an experience serves as a wake up call.

(Book ref. 2) *"All the Joy you can Stand"* by Debra Jackson Gandy "You have to retrieve your spirit from negative and unhealed memories and experiences, and relationships from your past, so that you can make use of the precious spiritual energy in the present."

(Bible ref. 1) Jeremiah 29:11,13 "For I know the plans I have for you declares the Lord. Plans to give you hope and a future. You will seek Me and find Me when you seek Me with all you heart."

Because of different religions in the world, seek whichever higher power does this for you. That is who you need to be seeking with all you heart. Apply "your soul power" spiritual coach when I refer to God and the universe and hopefully find a connection. Kindness, love, understanding, peace and integrity are universal!

(Daily Word ref. 2) "I trust God to lead me to those people and experiences that will bless my journey of knowing the joy of spiritual fulfillment."

(Bible ref. 2) Proverbs 4:23 "Above all else, guard your heart, for it is the wellspring of life."

Spirituality comes through you, not to you. God is in everything and is everywhere. Be forgiving, have patience, keep the door open and appreciate. Your dreams will be fulfilled and the world will be peaceful when you follow the divine order of the universe. Everything is provided in time and on time. It is up to each and everyone of us to seek our purpose and figure out what to do with what we are given. In return, we spread that purpose by loving and teaching others. Our purpose is to share with others. The universal windows are open for kindness, love, understanding, peace and integrity. When we have all these windows open, they will open the doors!

You'll welcome tests because you are aware that when you learn your tests, you have the power within to make choices that will serve your mind, body and soul well. You can't just say that you are a spiritual being and then not practice it. This would be the same thing as a person who goes to church once a week and the other six days he thinks he can do whatever. Your attitude and your thoughts on a daily basis is what forms how you feel about life. To grow spiritually is to think, feel and act in a kind manner to all, including self! Everything that happens to you has spiritual meaning. All lessons are stepping stones that bring you through the path of patience. In time, your unique individual character is formed. You concentrate on building bridges not walls.

Chapter 3

Formula/Assignment

The formula that we can apply to life is to find out our assignment from above, enjoy the ride, expect surprises. The universe loves to surprise us and watch us grow.

(Book ref. 3): by Billy Graham in *"Unto the Hills"*. "God's formulas are so simple that we ignore them because we think there must be more to it than that."

God "your soul power" has given you tools to use your talents. We need to ask God where He needs us and when He answers we need to go and do our best wherever He places us.

(Daily Word ref. 3) "Through an inner God-given creativity, I contribute in life every day. I am divinely inspired to be a continually renewed, ongoing expression of creativity."

We all are born equal and deserve all the abundance that life has to offer. All you have to do is ask, seek, knock.

First: ASK- What can I do? How can I be a solution? Where do you need me?

Second: SEEK- Read and be aware of lessons in everything you do. Pursue what you're here for. Stop, look, listen.

Third: KNOCK and say- "I'm ready for you to use me for your glory." "I'm ready to do what I was sent here to do."

Add: "This or something better for the good of all."

What will the answer be when you knock? Knock knock, the door is open – you already know who is there. If you asked and seeked – learned and paid attention – the life door is open for you for any and all possibilities. It's all up to you and your thoughts – no one else can do this for you. You are an original – not a copy.

(Bible ref. 3) Matthew 7:7-8 "Ask, and it will be given you; search, and you will find; knock, and the door will be opened for you. For everyone who asks receives, and everyone who searches finds, and for everyone who knocks, the door will be opened."

Don't just ask - what am I here for - what's the purpose of life? It is up to you, your responsibility, to go out and seek the answer. You need to find your assignment, then serve people with that assignment. You have to pursue happiness; it's not given to you. Believe in yourself and the universe.

You don't get what you want. You get what you need. Your prayers are always answered. Sometimes the answer isn't what you expected. Everything you need to do your assignment is given to you. Your responsibility is to find out what to do with what is given to you. Seek answers to how you can serve yourself and others with what you have. The universe is the given formula, and you are given what you need, but you have to do the work. That is the part that is not just given to you!! Your blessings are meant to be shared. Show your gratitude to the universe by sharing your blessings with others.

(Quote ref. 8) by Albert Schweitzer *"I don't know what your destiny will be, but one thing I do know; the only ones among you who will be happy are those who have sought and found how to serve."*

(Quote ref. 9) Benjamin Franklin – *"The Declaration Of Independence doesn't guarantee happiness, only the pursuit of it. You have to catch up with it yourself."*

(Lyrics ref. 1) *"Lord I Believe in You"*: "Though I can't see you with my eyes, deep in my heart your presence I find. And I'll keep my trust in you, no one can take this joy away."

Everything will flow in divine order. Go out of your comfort zone and do the things that you fear. You will be in awe when you find out all that you can do. Obstacles will come when you don't stop, look, listen. See what the obstacles are trying to tell you. They are there to test you and make you grow. Be aware of everything. You will have to learn patience. Things don't always come to you in the way you expect them to. Surprises are what the universe specializes in. Where do you think the term "oh my God" comes from? You're always surprised or relieved right before you say that, aren't you? In fact, more often then not, things come in very unexpected ways. It's important that before going to bed that you think of all the things that happened to you all day because maybe there was an unexpected surprise message that you overlooked. Look for blessings in the unexpected.

Now, I want to get one thing straight. Some of you might be thinking that you are going to be spending a lot of time analyzing everything. You don't need to pick everything apart. What you do need to do is practice empathy, patience and understanding. You need to be on the look out. Be aware of everything. Be aware of your environment. Be aware of other people and their feelings just like you should be of your own. Your life is certainly worth trying something that will benefit you and others! Take everything that you learn and put it into perspective. Seek the messages that are hidden in lessons throughout your life. There is always a lesson to be learned from every test given. Sort all the lessons of your life. All the pieces of your life. Put all pieces to good use. Collect all the puzzle pieces and put them all together. Ultimately everything joins in the end.

(Quote ref. 10) Jack Canfield writes; *"Roadblocks are put in your path to force you into a different path, a path that is truer to your real purpose. Even when you can't move forward, you can turn right or you can turn left, but you have to keep moving."*

We need to go beyond the surface and find out what the lesson is. A lesson is to be learned in everything that comes toward us. Life stands for (L) Learning (I) To inquire (F) Finding (E) Evolve. Learn the lessons, ask questions, seek in full pursuit about everything and anything, and unfold, develop, and change gradually. Learning never stops. Be in awe of everything just like a child. Even if you think you know something already, look again for the broader sense of everything.

There is a *reason* for everything. We must take everything a step further. Find the reason for that book popping out from the shelf saying "get me." Do that thing that you are so propelled to do. That inner voice is there for a reason. Worship is personal. We should help each other out, be loving, caring, promote understanding and be open minded, but we all need to have solitude time and do what nourishes our mind, body and soul. Meditate and listen for messages. Pray and take zen time or moment to moment awareness. We need to become healed and whole and have a good relationship with ourselves.

The only one that is responsible for your life and happiness is you. Listen to one another, everyones stories. We are all connected, but also realize that each one of us has to go through their own lessons and learn from them. We help one another by listening to one another, but we also have to think for ourselves. Life is a balancing act. Just like everything in life, apply moderation. Easy does it and everything will all come together for the good of all concerned. What works wonderful for one person might stifle another. Keep trying, never give up. Never lose the wonder of life. Laugh often with others and yourself. It truly is a wonderful world.

(Lyrics ref. 2) "*What a Wonderful World*" - "The bright blessed day. The dark sacred night. And I think to myself, what a wonderful world."

Now, get a pen because you will be doing some homework, I mean life work. After each section are blank pages "*my journal time*" which is your journal time. This is where you will put all your feelings and thoughts about issues covered in this book and how you will make changes in your life, if need be. It will be a record of your progress, sort of a cross between a diary and an agreement contract with yourself. It will be a list of things you need to work on to live your life to its fullest. Now stretch and take a deep breath and...

(Lyrics ref. 3) "*Get down tonight*" - "Do a little dance, make a little love, get down tonight."

Dance with your mind, body and soul. Love yourself by finally getting to and getting down to improving you life.

Remember that the *"My Journal Time"* is for you to write. You need to reach inside yourself in order to make things work for you. Sometimes when you write things out you will find hidden trouble spots that will surface. Take care of these issues so that the healing process can be enforced. You are here to find what your calling is. Also, it is your responsibility to find out what your purpose here is and blaming others or past circumstances are not options. You can rethink your way of thinking right now. Before we continue I would like to say: After careful concentration and awareness to everything you listen to, watch or read, it is up to you to delete, weed out, what does not serve you. Keep only what will nourish you to grow into someone you would like to be around. Be open minded and know yourself well and by all means...

(Quote ref. 11) by William Shakespeare *"To thine ownself be true."*

My dad wrote that quote in my high school year book and I never forgot it.

Change your life around today. Not someday, not later, but today. The sooner you figure out this buddies with the universe formula, the fuller your life will become. It doesn't matter what our assignment is. No assignment is too small. We are all very significant on the wheel of life. Be the best cog that you can be and be sure you are serving yourself and others. As long as your occupation gives you a feeling of well being and you are not hurting anyone, then you are benefitting yourself and others. Your mental, physical, emotional, spiritual health and being of service to others is the only thing that really matters.

Chapter 4

What Is This Now?
(My mother's favorite saying)

✦

The Teen Years To 100 Plus

Read each and every age. Don't skip to your age. You might have missed a step somewhere along your journey. Read past your age to see that you always have something to look forward to. Learn, relearn and sometimes un-learn. Get your life together. Doesn't matter what your age is.

(Quote ref.12) by Francis Picabia *"Our heads are round so that our thoughts can change direction."*

Uh, oh – what is this now? Just when you thought you had problems, puberty steps in. Now you have two things that have run amok, thoughts and hormones. Again you would get advice from what people think, mostly confusing, with a lot of ifs ands or buts added and the dreaded deal with it. We need to understand that everyone is doing the best that they know how at a given time in their life. No one is on the exact same road as you are. What you experience at 10, someone else might not experience until they are 20 or never at all. Everyone learns from the tests given to them and learn at their own pace. Life is a process and a journey with many roads to choose from. When you hit roadblocks accept them as challenges to learn something from.

Most things in life are not as bad as they seem. Sometimes just a good rest will help you see things more clearly. Go within, meditate and listen for messages. Talk to someone who is a good listener. Pray for guidance.

(Lyrics ref. 4) *"Let it be"* - "When I find myself in times of trouble, Mother Mary comes to me, speaking words of wisdom, let it be. There will be an answer, let it be."

Sometimes you just have to sit back and listen. Take time out and continue.

(Lyrics ref. 5) *"Ooh-oo child"* - "Ooh-oo child, things are gonna get easier. Ooh-oo child things'll get brighter. We'll put it all together and will get it all done. When your head is much lighter, we'll walk in the rays of a beautiful sun."

Say no to peer pressures. Love of self and life are permanent highs. Drugs, alcohol, joy rides, food, hoarding, shopping, gambling and sex are temporary highs. Be responsible for yourself today so that you will have a future tomorrow. No one and nothing can give you love or make you see what a wonderful world this is except for you and your thoughts. Don't get in the habit of getting addicted to people. Learn to be your own idol. It's not considered selfish to look out for your best interests as long as you are not hurting anyone in the process.

Never give up searching and remember the journey is supposed to be savored. Visit your childhood often and the past, but just to peek in. Have an open mind to re-learn lessons but don't dwell there. Re-learn and then go forward. Live in the present moment.

(Quote ref.13) Leo Buscaglia wrote: *"Life is uncharted territory. It reveals its story one moment at a time."*

The future will take care of itself when the timing is right. This doesn't mean you just sit and wait, however. You do have to go on with life. You need to learn lessons and then apply those lessons to everyday life. Don't get into the blame business and always remember we are all here trying to find our way no matter what our age. You have choices and you have responsibilities. Choose wisely because your life is what you make it.

(Quote ref. 14) Grandma Moses wrote: *"Life is what you make it. Always has been, always will be."*

Always stop, look and listen. We learned this advice at three and it is one childhood lesson you should visit often throughout your life.

Pretend that you are a computer. An enormous filing cabinet of what you have put into your mind. Absorb everything you can. Go within yourself everyday just like you go into your computer. If what you believed yesterday to be true the next day, then file it in your mind. If something does not serve your beliefs any longer, you can either put it in the back of your mind for reference or you can delete it. Be the master drive of your mind. Your thoughts have been programed in but can always be re-programed just like your computer.

(Quote ref. 15) Ralph Waldo Emerson wrote: *"Trust thyself. Nothing is at last sacred but the integrity of your own mind."*

We are all in the same boat, but going different directions because we are all unique. We can help others paddle but everyone needs to steer the boat in the direction that benefits them at a given time. Listen to the advice of others but weed out what will not serve you. You can even try some of the advice. Be open minded. Keep your ears and eyes open for snakes in the grass (people or things that can't be trusted). These are obstacles that are trying to teach you something. Don't ignore the snakes or the wolves. Find out why they are in your life and then make changes. Keep doors open for communication with those who you feel safe with. Stop, look and listen to see if it's the right charted course for you.

Since I brought up the snake in the grass issue, I would like to add this. It's ok to be as shrewd as a snake as long as you are using this brain usage for the good of all concerned. After all, the snake is one of Gods creatures. If someone else is being a snake in the grass to you, don't think of the snake as being the problem. Think of it as being the solution to learning a lesson and then go forward from there. Beware of the snakes in the grass and seek reasons for their presence. Be aware, consciously informed and beware, cautious and wary of the snake. But by all means, never ignore the snake. This of course goes for sly foxes and ravenous wolves too.

There was a little rhyme years ago that went like this: "Love many, trust few, always paddle your own canoe."

(Quote ref. 16) Jack Canfield writes *"Most of life is on the job training. Some of the most important things can only be learned in the process of doing them."*

Honor your mind, body and soul and feed them right. Get on a good nutritional plan and exercise program. There are plenty of tasty nutritional alternatives to junk food. Not only will your body thank you and serve you well but so will your mind and soul. Also feed your mind good positive thoughts. Everything is totally connected. Meditate and go within everyday to keep your soul fed. Taking preventative steps now will serve you well throughout your entire life. When you have your health you have just about everything. We are all here to find our assignment, our work or our calling.

(Quote ref. 17) by Rumi: *"Everyone has been made for some particular work and the desire for that work has been put in his (or her) heart."*

When you are in your 20's, confusion takes over again. You have gained some knowledge of life but not sure what to do with it. You have lots of doubts, laugh a lot usually just to fit in. You cry some, worry about money and think about your future. There is a lot of experimentation but then you realize you don't get very good results like you did in science class. Again, addictions are only temporary highs and not solutions. Some of us get stuck in this rut for a long long time because we don't understand that these obstacles are presented to us to think more. We would rather escape into an addiction and hope it goes away. It's a quick fix that can prove to be a nightmare further down the road. We get ourselves into more of a mess by going around instead of through. Addictions rob our mind, body, and soul of nutrients and keep us in a mode of shoulda, woulda, coulda which is highly unproductive.

(Quote ref.18) Ringo Starr (one of the Beatles) wrote: *"I hope the fans will take up meditation instead of drugs."*

(Daily Word ref. 4) " Through meditation and prayer, I open a wellspring of divine ideas that prospers and blesses me."

(Quote ref. 19) by Abraham Maslow *"If our true nature is permitted to guide our life, we grow healthy, fruitful, and happy."*

Love of self and life are permanent highs. You will reach this permanent high in as long or short of time as you choose. Either you "get it" now or you "wait" until your life passes before you. The choice is yours and it's totally your responsibility. No matter what your life entailed up to this point you can change at any time. Don't worry about the whys of yesterday, the hows of today, the whens of tomorrow. (Whys?) Because you needed to learn something. (Hows?) By applying what you learn to your life the best way you know. (Whens?) When you have used every puzzle piece of your life and applied them to fill the needs for the good of all those concerned.

(Quote ref. 20) Ralph Waldo Emerson - *"What lies behind us and what lies before us are small matters compared to what lies within us."*

Like in the song:

(Lyrics ref. 6) *"Return to Innocence"* – "That's not the beginning of the end. That's the return to yourself. The return to innocence. Just look into your heart my friend."

Visit, take peeks into your childhood and the past often but not to seek pity or to find blame or to judge. No one likes a pity party. Get off you pity pot. What you need to do is find out your strengths and re-learn lessons or even un-learn things that no longer serve you. Be open minded and understand that everyone is really trying to do the best they can from what they have learned from their lessons. Unforgiving, judgment and blame are unproductive.

(Bible ref. 4) Matthew 6:14-15 - "For if you forgive men their trespasses, your heavenly Father will also forgive you. But if you do not forgive men their trespasses, neither will your Father forgive your trespasses."

Do not be revengeful.

(Quote ref. 21) by May Maloo; *"The only people with whom you should try to get even, are those who have helped you."*

Find compassion for those you feel have harmed you in some way or have stifled you. Forgiveness heals everyone. Everyone has good days and bad days. It's sad but true that sometimes we just get caught up in the crossfire and someone speaks words of anger to us or vice versa. True, some things should never be said but if they are, try to work it out with the person. If you can't, then see if there was a lesson to be learned and then move on. I got a card from my son Jake recently that played music:

(Lyrics ref. 7) *"Mama Said"* - "Mama said there'd be days like this. Hey! Don't you worry."

There are good days and bad days but always something to learn from each day. Also from:

(Quote ref. 22) Zora Neale Hurston *"There are years that ask questions and years that answer."*

Then you hit the 30 mark. Maybe career isn't taking off in the direction you thought it would. You might be married now and have a family. Savor the moments and live in the present. Be sure you are on the right path and if you need to make changes, do so. You always have the choice to change. Take lots of solitude journeys into your mind and have deep conversations with yourself. Always keep faith and love in your thoughts. Now, this is especially for you guys reading this. You do have feelings. Macho went out a long time ago. If you want to cry, cry. Let your feelings be known. There is an excellent book out for you guys:

(Book ref. 4) *"Fire in the Belly"* – by Sam Keen: "At no time in history have there been so many men looking for new roles, new attitudes, and new ways of being." "I must take time to be with myself, to discover my desires, my rhythms, my tastes, my gifts, my hopes, my wounds. We need solitude to keep the relationship between me, myself, and I alive and growing."

The female version is listed under experiences/temptations section in this book and is written by Marianne Willliamson. Both are excellent sources and both should be read by all.

Age 30 is the age where you're past the wild find yourself 20's and you really start thinking about your life and relationships. If you are under the age of 30 right now, then re-read age 20. Don't miss any parts. You may be able to make the 30's a smoother ride for yourself. If you believe you need to make a big change because of a relationship issue, always remember this: Everybody deserves to be loved fully. If you are in a relationship that is not working out for some reason and can't bring yourself to break it off (you care too much about the person) but there are issues unresolvable, staying in it because you think you will hurt the other is actually hurting both of you. You are hurting the other more if you stay with them and are not giving yourself fully in the relationship. You are not moving on and the other is being deceived by you. Keep communication open and maybe you will find out that they want to move on too.

(Lyrics ref. 8) "*Neither one of us*" - "So we just go on (we go on) hurting and pretending and convincing ourselves to give it just one more try (one more try). Because neither one of us wants to be the first to say farewell my love, goodbye (goodbye.)"

If you are in an abusive relationship, meaning any relationship that is toxic to your mind, body and/or soul, get out now! This of course goes for any age group! Bad behavior in any form is unacceptable. You always have the choice to leave. There are many resources out there for you to get help.

(Lyrics ref. 9) "*Circle of Life*" – "In the circle of life, It's the wheel of fortune. It's the leap of faith. It's the band of hope. Till we find our place. On the path unwinding."

(Quote ref. 23) by Aristotle "*Where your talents and the needs of the world cross, there lies your vocation.*"

40's coming up fast. I can almost see the hill. Where has my life gone (you ask) oh yeah, over the hill. Remember to stay on the top of the hill for awhile and enjoy the scenery and hang out with nature. Decide what to do for the next 50+ years.

(Quote ref. 24) Frank Lloyd Wright writes: " *I believe in God, only I spell it nature.*"

Always remember you can make plans but don't get too attached to the details.

(Bible ref. 5) Proverbs 19:21 "The human mind may devise many plans, but it is the purpose of the Lord that will be established."

The details belong to God.

Make a list of things that you always wanted to do but haven't yet. Dig deep into your soul and meditate on what you could do to make your life more in tune with your dreams.

(Quote ref. 25) Blaise Pascal - *"All of mans' problems stem from his inability to sit in a room quietly by himself."*

Again, if you need to make changes, do so.

(Lyrics ref. 10) *"His love is coming over me"* – "I don't question this moment. I won't hesitate no more. We'd be fools not to jump in with both feet."

Also (Quote ref. 26) by Eleanor Roosevelt *"The future belongs to those who believe in the beauty of their dreams."*

Bob Seger sings a song about when you were18 and approaching 40:

(Lyrics ref. 11) *"Like a rock"* - "Twenty years now. Where'd they go? Twenty years I don't know. I sit and wonder sometimes where they've gone."

You only have so much time here. Learn how to live life to the fullest.

(Quote ref. 27) by George Bernard Shaw: *"The people who get on in this world are the people who get up and look for the circumstances they want, and, if they can't find them, make them."*

(Quote ref. 28) by Helen Keller *"One cannot consent to creep when one has the desire to soar."*

Oh no, say it isn't so. Is that a candle marked with a 50 on my cake? Now is the time to mount that hill. Better yet, make it a mountain. Perch on the peak of mount think. You're less than half way through your life. Put your thinking cap on and if you haven't been doing things you enjoy, why not? What are you waiting for? Some day is today, right now, this moment. Read under my 60's section for ideas and keep that mind, body and soul active.

(Lyrics ref. 12) *"Up where we belong"* - "Lord lift us up where we belong. Where the eagles cry on a mountain high."

Did that person just ask me for my senior citizen card? Remember this is just a label. Being 60 means get those dancing shoes on, or those golf, bowling, or any sports shoes on, even skis. How about putting a good pair of walking shoes on and keep that bod and mind moving. Staying active keeps mind, body and soul alive. Just forget 50 being the new 30 and make 60 to 100+young the new 30!!

In the lyrics from:

(Lyrics ref. 13) *"Can you feel the love tonight"* – from The Lion King we are told: "Theres a calm surrender to the rush of day. An enchanted moment and it sees me through."

Make every moment count. Forget age, statistics, what you should be doing in your *"senior years"* or any of those insane labels.

If you've always wanted to travel, go now	Rent/buy DVD'S on travel
Join clubs	Do volunteer work
Write a book	Paint/draw
Be a mentor	Help children
Be a consultant	Swim
Skinny dip	Fish
Jet ski	Golf
Open a small business	Go camping
Part time job (enjoyable)	Make/sell arts/crafts
Dance	Sing or compose
Go biking	Hike

Get a pet	Bowl
Give lessons	Take lessons
Scrapbooking	Play
Sew	Do woodworking
Do yoga or tai chi	Cook world fare
Skate	Garden
Listen to music	Go to the theater/concerts
Go to museums	Go to zoos
Boating	Horseback riding
Read more	Play cards
Play trivia games	Play checkers/chess
Crossword puzzles	Board games
Do jigsaw puzzles	Do mental teasers
Learn pampering skills	Learn relaxing skills

You may think you can't do some of the things mentioned above, but try some, you might be surprised at what you can do and might feel a lot better too. I haven't lost my mind, I know I'm writing in the 60's section. The 60's is the new 30's, remember? So are the 70's to 100+. The library has a wellspring of information and you can check out more than books. They have music, dvd's, video cassettes, audio books etc. You can sign up for classes that they offer and they have computers that you can use. What ever you decide to do, just do it. Connect mind, body and soul in everything you do.

(Quote ref. 29) by Shirley Lord – *"Age is totally unimportant. The years are really irrelevant. It's how you cope with them."*

Or how about this.

(Quote ref. 30) by Satenig St. Marie *"We can go into quiet retirement, which is the traditional stereotype of a 65-year old, or we can take a risk and put ourselves out where the action is."*

Don't take pills that have a zillion and one side effects. What's the sense to that, people? Why do you want to be a part of a domino effect? Read and learn about health and nutrition and find all the natural alternatives. Don't get on the pill wagon. There are no quick fixes. Remember what you read in my 20's section? We all are responsible for our own bodies. Find alternatives to taking medications. It's never to late to start a good nutritional and exercise program. Read up on ailments that can be reversed and remember, your mind, body and soul work together. Go to your mind and ask yourself if your bodies pain and or disease could be caused by your thoughts. Are you a negative or positive person? Are you upset? Are you treating yourself right in every way, shape and form? If not, why not?

Seek professional medical assistance with anything you don't understand about alternative medicine. Also, taking preventative steps in the first place will eliminate many ailments from occurring. This again falls under being totally responsible for yourself. The best cure is to prevent it in the first place.

Oh boy – now you're 70 to 100+ and full of lessons, wisdom, experience, but no one wants your opinion. Everyone just thinks you're an old fartin senile fool. This is the time to share and tell you're stories. Keep doing the things that you can, do the things you enjoy. Re-read the 60's section for ideas. You are at the point now where these lyrics really make sense:

(Lyrics ref. 14) *"From a distance"* – "And the eagle takes to flight, and it echoes through the land. Marching in a common band. Playing songs of hope. Playing songs of peace. They are the songs of every man."

No matter what your age, be sure you have the three L's in your life: Love, laugh and learn.

(Quote ref. 31) Sophia Loren *"There is a fountain of youth: it is your mind, your talents, the creativity you bring to your life and the lives of people you love. When you learn to tap this source, you will truly have defeated age."*

My son Jake gave me a card a couple of years ago where he wrote that I should do something special for my self on my birthday. He wrote that it had been a great year of change and that there are many more to come (50) more. I sure hope he's right because that will put me at 100 + years young. Embrace your life with childlike joy, compassion and imagination.

(Quote ref. 32) by Victor Borge: *"Laughter is the shortest distance between two people."*

There are a couple of pages to write *"My Journal Time"*. Write things down that you are starting to work on. Remember to start each issue with for example: I am working on better nutrition by... and my mind, body and soul are healthy and strong. Not, I will start working on better nutrition by. These are like your affirmations and should always be written *as if* you are already doing something or *as if* something is already happening. Also, write about things that you agree with me on and disagree with me on. Always ask yourself *why* and answer from your heart. Dig deep down and pull out your feelings. Come up with solutions of your own that will serve both yourself and others. Always end each of *"My Journal Time"* sessions with "this or something better for the good of all concerned".

Start of *"My Journal Time"*.

How do I feel about all of this and why? My list of things I am working on are...

My Journal

My Journal

My Journal

Something else to do: visionary therapy. Get a bunch of old magazines. If you don't have any old magazines around, you can get them at thrift stores, rummage sales, used library book sales or friends. They usually sell for a dime or a quarter. You can also draw, paint, use greeting cards, postcards, catalogs, computer images. Cut out pictures of things you enjoy and things you would like to do. Cut out words that describe you or describe what you would like to do. For instance, my collage has people riding bikes, dancing, listening to music, reading, an angel, a picture that says God bless our home, a heart with the word family in it, mountain and travel scenes, swimming, laying in a hammock, someone meditating, walking on the beach, a motor home, food that I like, gardening, and words like: Harmony, Music, Serenity, Simplicity, Family, Travel, Laugh, Dream, Healing, Odyssey, Fruit of the Spirit (love, joy, peace), and on and on it goes. Don't limit yourself with what you enjoy. Dig deep down for who you really are, not who you think you should be or what society thinks.

If you really want to get creative, you can use real items. Do you like the beach? Paste sand and shells on the collage. Like to garden? Use packets of seed or the seeds themselves, a pair of gloves and tools. Craft person? Paste buttons, material, tools, wood, whatever. Like to putter in the garage? Paste nails, wood, electric supplies, small car parts. You can use toys for this or items from craft stores. Are you a designer? Paste writing tools, portfolios, blueprints, computer programs. Like to cook? Paste on pasta, cooking utensils, recipes. If you do go this route, paste everything on a board instead of poster board for more sturdiness.

Get your self a piece of poster cardboard or piece of wood and paste/nail/staple everything on it in a mod podge way collage. Hang it up where you will see it everyday. If you always have been a negative person, now is the time to change that pattern and be positive!! Visualize and reprogram your thoughts. You can also add real photos of yourself and others doing things you enjoy, to remind you to keep doing them. Take time to find things, at least a month or two so you have everything you want on it before placing them on the board. The purpose is to get you inspired. Visualize it every day. Put your intentions out there and the universe will take care of the details.

Chapter 5

Experiences

First of all – get it through to yourself that life is a series of experiences, lessons, tests. You will not be able to go to any further experiences unless you pass the previous test. Well, actually you are able to, but you won't get anywhere. It's kind of like rocking in a rocking chair. It gives you something to do but it doesn't get you anywhere. You will get stuck or just keep rocking in the same way over and over and never learning the lesson and never applying it to everyday life.

(Quote ref. 33) Gail Sheehy writes: *"To be tested is good. The challenged life may be the best therapist."*

(Daily Word ref. 5) "A new experience will arise out of each new situation. I look forward to the upcoming event, knowing that it will be harmonious and beneficial for all."

(Book ref. 5) *"The Pilgrimage"* by Paulo Coelho -"Everything you have learned up to now makes sense only if it is applied in real life. Wisdom has value only if it helps us to overcome some obstacle."

This is where the terms "stuck in a rut, I keep making the same mistakes, or I seem to be stuck in the same pattern when it comes to relationships" come in. Experiences will keep being repeated until you "get it". Even then it is not over, because you will then be tested by temptations just to be sure you learned something from the experience.

Experiences can make you better or bitter. Try to go with becoming better. An only child can become selfish (bitter) or will share freely and become (better.) Children from a large family can become selfish (bitter) by hoarding as an adult because they didn't have as a child.

They can become giving (better) because they learned to share as a child. No one, I repeat, no one, has an excuse for anything. It's all in how you learn from your experiences and what kind of life you want to make for yourself.

Abused as a child or adult? First, get help. Second, forgive the abuser and forgive yourself. Third, go through stages of healing. Fourth, break the chain and help others.

(Quote ref. 34) by James Joyce: *"Welcome life! I go to encounter for the millionth time the reality of experience."*

(Book ref. 6) *"You can heal your life"* by Louise Hay, she says "We are each responsible for all of our experiences."

(Book ref. 7) *"If life is a game, these are the rules"* by Cherie Carter-Scott, one of the 10 rules is "There are no mistakes, only lessons".

This is a very important point. A mistake is defined as an error. A lesson is defined as anything learned by study or experience. Taking this a step further, error is wrong doing, offense. To study means to carefully understand and consider. Experience is a process of learning by personally observing, testing, or doing something. Taking this another step, offense is an attack or cause of uneasiness, displeasure and anxiety. Observing means being mindful and taking notice to details.

Lesson

Learning by study or experience and after careful consideration and understanding of your observing, testing and/or doing something, you become mindful to a situation.

Mistake

Making error and doing wrong and being offensive, attacking and having feelings of uneasiness, displeasure or anxiety. As you can see, lessons put you into a mode for positivity and mistakes put you into a mode of negativity. Don't say I made a mistake, say, I learned a lesson.

Temptations

Even back in biblical days they had temptations. Who could forget the dreaded snake in the Garden Of Eden?

(Bible ref. 6) Genesis 3 : Snake says; "You will not surely die."

Eve took a risk. Personally I think that this was a good thing. Risk is good. We should all be thanking Eve instead of blaming her. Paradise is heaven but we are here on earth to live! Adam and Eve had a choice and took free will. This gave man the freedom to choose and be more like God and know good and evil. If we know no pain, how will we recognize peace and joy? All the characters in the Bible went out of their comfort zones and became stronger. The trick is to find out which temptations will serve you and others well and which ones will not. At any rate, learn from your lessons and move forward.

(Bible ref. 7) Matthew 7:15; There are the wolves dressed in sheep's clothing. This too keeps us on our toes. Makes us stay on track and stop, look and listen. Learn the lessons from the snakes and wolves and then move on.

(Book ref. 8) "*A Womans Worth*" by Marianne Williamson. She writes about toxic relationships and the healing process and how you are tested. Note: Since her book is about women, she writes about recovering from attraction to dangerous men. If you are a guy reading this, it also applies to dangerous women. Also, if you are a guy, you should read her book so you understand women more clearly. Gals, you should read Sam Keens book as well, as I described earlier. Marianne says "When you're really ill, you don't even know a snake when you see one. Once recovery begins, you see a snake and you know it's a snake, but you still play with it. Once you've landed in true recovery zone, you see a snake, you know it's a snake, and you cross to the other side of the road."

The point is, there are lessons to be learned and temptations will be used to make you aware. The universe will stop at nothing to get you to learn something. Of course your choices and your awareness will determine the extent of your repeated lessons. There is a saying that has been around for a long time. " You're either a part of the problem or the solution."

If you are "stuck in a rut" for a long time and you are not making an effort to get out of your rut, then you are either getting something out of the situation or you fear going out on a limb and changing. You can stay here as long as you want. It's your choice when you want to change.

(Book ref. 8) Marianne Williamson says "We suffer according to the level of our bullshit."

Cause And Effect

Cause and effect is well looking into. You basically do not have any control over anything but your thoughts and how you respond to something. If someone bugs you then you still have open wounds to resolve or need to learn a new way to express yourself. The only way you can change the effect something is having on you is to change your reaction. My daughter Jenny use to say "They bug me but I love um." She was expressing that because she loved her brothers she could deal with the bugging and it was as simple as that. Out of the mouths of babes.

(Quote ref. 35) by Eleanor Roosevelt; *"You have to accept whatever comes and the only important thing is that you meet it with the best you have to give."*

(Quote ref. 36) by Elisabeth Kubler-Ross; *"I believe that we are solely responsible for our choices, and we have to accept the consequences of every deed, word, and thought throughout our lifetime."*

Communicating with an open mind and having a non assuming attitude is a must. Don't get caught into the blame business. Blame can only lead to a tit for tat unproductive path for all concerned.

(Quote ref. 37) Aldous Huxley; *" Experience is not what happens to a man. It is what a man does with what happens to him."*

My daughter Jenny gave me a card a couple of years ago that had things that a mom is remembered for. She added her own to it under the cards (assorted words of wisdom section). She wrote: "Stop that, or you'll suffer the consequences." I guess she was listening to my cause and effect lectures after all.

We reap what we sow – is the best comparison of cause and effect. If you have positive thoughts than you will receive positivty in your life. Like will attract like. Plant the seed by asking for ideas to get closer to your talent and the money will come after serving others with that talent. Don't say "I want money" or " I want to marry rich." These statements will put you into the selfish loophole mode – which is in the movie *Bedazzled*. Don't ask for anything that has a selfish reason attached to it. We are here to bring new ideas to our God given talents. We then serve others with this and then receive the reward, the blessings. Than we are still tested – to see what we do with what we receive.

Wisdom

(Quote ref. 38) by Sandra Carey *"Never confuse knowledge with wisdom. One helps you earn a living, the other helps you build a life."*

To me - wisdom is the understanding of knowledge and acting on it in everyday life. Wisdom works with spirituality by applying faith – discipline and the unfolding into one with God and one another. Wisdom is the follow through stage – the I am ready to be the student stage. Wisdom is the going beyond knowledge stage. It's inner knowledge – it's awareness and understanding.

(Bible ref. 8) Proverbs 3:13 "Happy are those who find wisdom, and those who get understanding."

I've overheard many times when people are talking about someones situation that somewhere along our upbringing we seem to think that so called educated people should know everything. A comment might go something like this: Did you hear about so in-so? He got himself in a real mess – I thought he had brains. Wisdom is not based on how well of an education you have. If you don't have understanding or awareness to life itself, then you are just walking around with a bunch of degrees and are basically a robot. More on this under awareness.

You have to apply what you learn to everyday life - otherwise it is all for naught. An ignorant person is defined as: unaware, uninformed, ignores. Even if you can't read or write (you're illiterate) you are still aware, informed, and notice things.

(Quote ref. 39) Like Maya Angelou says: *"My mother said that I must always be intolerant of ignorance but understanding of illiteracy. That some people, unable to go to school, were more educated and more intelligent than college professors."*

Take in all the experiences you can but always remember to form sound judgments on your experiences and apply your wisdom to everyday life. Wisdom entails compassion and putting everything you learn into action. Here is a story that fits well here:

(Book ref. 9) *"Why your life sucks"* by Alan Cohen; "The fisherman story: An American businessman stood at the pier of a small coastal Mexican village when a small boat with just one fisherman docked. Inside the boat were several large yellow fin tuna. The American complimented the Mexican on the quality of his fish and asked how long it took to catch them.

The Mexican replied, "Only a little while."

The American then asked, "Why don't you stay out longer and catch more fish?"

The fisherman answered, "I have enough to support my family's immediate needs."

The businessman then asked, "But what do you do with the rest of your time?"

The fisherman answered, "I sleep late, fish a little, play with my children, take a siesta with my wife, stroll into the village each evening where I sip wine and play guitar with my amigos. I have a full and busy life, senor."

The American scoffed, "I am a Harvard M.B.A. and I can help you. You should spend more time fishing, and with the income buy a bigger boat. With the proceeds from the bigger boat you could buy several boats, and eventually you would own a fleet of fishing boats.

Instead of selling your catch to a middleman, you could sell directly to the processor and eventually open your own cannery. You would control the product, processing, and distribution. You would need to leave this small coastal fishing village and move to Mexico City, then L.A., and eventually New York City where you will run your expanding enterprise."

The fisherman asked, "But senor, how long will this all take?"

The American replied, "15-20 years."

"But what then senor?"

The American laughed and said, "Thats the best part! When the time is right you would announce an IPO and sell your company stock to the public and become very rich-you would make millions."

"Millions, senor? Then what?"

"Then you would retire. Move to a small coastal fishing village where you would sleep late, fish a little, play with your kids, take siesta with your wife, stroll to the village in the evenings where you could sip wine and play your guitar with your amigos."

See what I mean? – Awareness – Harvard man lacked putting his knowledge into proper perspective. Be sure you know where you are going in life. You may already be there or at least have the wisdom to get there.

(Quote ref. 40) by Elbert Hubbard *"It is much better to have common sense without an education than to have education without common sense."*

(Lyrics ref. 15) *"All about love"* - "We've got CD sets and videos, radio and TV shows...We've got books and magazines to read on everything from A to Z...But I hope with all this information buzzing through our brains – That we will not let our hearts forget the most important thing – Is love, love, love, love, love."

As you go through your experiences always be aware of everything. Sometimes – in fact more often than not – there is a hidden message. Be sure that you always love your fellow man/woman (person), nature, and environment, by showing respect, compassion and empathy. Remember that you are here to serve others and even though we all have to go through our own experiences – we need to share our experiences-put your experiences out there for others. Others can get ideas on how to bring themselves to a more fulfilling life. We are all teachers and students. Our days are numbered – we can't learn everything we need to know – without the help of others.

EXPERIENCES: Keep tract of your experiences and your attitudes toward them in *"My Journal Time"*. Do you welcome them? If not – why? Take note of how your experiences make you feel. What have you learned from experiences recently and are you aware of others feelings and things in your environment? Could you learn to respond differently to certain situations in order to have better relationships and outcomes? Are you bullshitting yourself and/or others and why? Are you stuck in a rut – why? Do you apply your lessons to your life? HOW?

My Journal

My Journal

My Journal

Chapter 6

Thoughts

(Quote ref. 41) by Dale Carnegie *"Happiness does not depend on what you are or have; it only depends on what you think."*

Some people think that if they have *things* they will be happy. Years ago people didn't have much but what they did have they appreciated and took care of. We had an older home one time in Wisconsin. The closets were very small and it dawned on me that people didn't need big closets. They had a couple of clothes and didn't have a lot of things to (store away) – really – how much do we need? We are mixed up with what we need/want. Also, people that I have known that were very well to do – had a lot of stuff - were not that happy. Personally I'm happier with less. Simplicity is much less stressful – less is better. Thoughts make us unique. We are our thoughts.

We talk to ourselves about 50,000 times a day. Always be sure that all of those thoughts are positive so that you will move forward in life in a productive way. Be sure that all of your thoughts are self nourishing - as well as – for the good of all others concerned. When negativity is around you – your heart and whole body will tell you what's working and what's not – all you have to do is be aware. When you feel drained you are probably in a negative environment. Your mind, body and soul never lie.

(Daily Word ref. 6) "I let each of my thoughts, words, and actions be a powerful force for love, for possibility, for opportunity, prosperity, for health."

One rainy day while thinking of what order to put chapters in this book, I came up with a little experiment based on just 1 thought – a word. I closed my eyes and said to myself, "Self, give me a word to let my thoughts go on a journey." The first word that rolled off my mind was rain. Now I guess that happened because it was raining out. I don't know and I don't care. Like I used to say when I was 9 - "Who cares" only the R was silent because I couldn't say my R's, so it came out "Who kaz." Some things just don't matter – sometimes you just have to go with the flow.

As I started thinking of the word rain, I started thinking of song lyrics. Lyrics have always been like a hobby of mine. As you can see – from previous pages - I like to remember lyrics from songs to fit situations. So, if I would be walking on the ocean with someone and they said : "The high tide is coming in." I might start to sing from the song:

(Lyrics ref. 16) *"Strollin on the water"* - "Let me rise above the high tide – I can do it, yeah – I know where my strength comes from."

It's a neat hobby. You help your mind to think of some certain song lyrics – body to dance and soul by inspiring lyrics. So here I am with the word rain. I started thinking of the song:

(Lyrics ref. 17) *"Singing in the rain"* - "I'm singing in the rain – just singing in the rain. What a glorious feeling – I'm happy again. I'm dancing and singing in the rain."

Then my mind went immediately to Dancing With The Stars TV show – One of the couples danced to this song. So naturally I got up and started dancing. Next my thoughts went to *rainy days and mondays always get me down.* Not sure why my mind went from happy to sad but I went with the flow once again. I thought of how tragic it was that a journalist commented on Karen Carpenters weight and it caused her such pain and then to anorexia and eventually to her death. My thought went one step further to all the other people who have eating disorders sometimes (and way to often) based on what society expects and what a lot of advertisers preach. And what do we do? Some of us go and add insult to injury with stares and jokes. If only we could get through to them that no one has the right to intimidate them.

(Quote ref. 42) Eleanor Roosevelt wrote: *"No one can make you feel inferior without your consent."*

Raindrops keep falling on my head from Butch Cassidy and the Sundance Kid was next on my mind. It stopped raining now so I decided to go for a bike ride – not on the handle bars though - like in the movie. Then my mind drifted off to Noahs Ark, you know, the 40 days and nights of rain. I got out my Bible and re-read the story. That made me think of sowing and reaping. I looked up sow in the Bible and it took me to:

(Bible ref. 9) Psalm 126 and sowing tears and reaping joy. This took me to seeds and how much they need to be nourished by the rain so they can become nourishing food for our bodies. It's amazing how little seeds can become vegetables, fruit and grains not to forget the beautiful flowers and trees. We also have seeds of our minds that grow from the impossible to the possible and of course the seeds that grow into human beings, animals, etc. Wow, all of this and I could go on and on. All from one word thought.

A very important point here. This was not just an experiment of thoughts. After I wrote them down, I soon realized I comforted my mind, body and soul during the experiment. I used my mind to think of the lyrics and various information. I then nourished my body by dancing and riding my bike and my soul by going to the bible and saying a prayer for those that still allow others to intimidate them. Later, I made myself a bowl of fruit and some brown rice after thinking of the seeds again. I took my bowl down by the bridge in my yard and enjoyed the nature. This was all good for my mind, body and soul. I felt totally connected and whole with my self, nature and the environment. This experiment made me aware that once again, there is no one like me in the whole world. I am a creation of God and those thoughts came from me. No one can take them away. It was just me – myself and I. No competition, no rules, no contest, naught, nothing.

(Daily Word ref. 7) "Pure joy comes with celebrating our unique differences. Each individual we meet has the potential to express all manner of God-given gifts, and we can help support and encourage the expression of such gifts."

Go ahead and do the experiment yourself. Even use the same word – rain – if you want. After that, close your eyes and ask for your own word and see what journey it takes you on. Enjoy and see if it all connects and if you use your mind, body and soul.

(Quote ref. 43) by James Allen. *"You are today where your thoughts have brought you; You will be tomorrow where your thoughts take you."*

(Quote ref. 44) by Buddha. *"Do not believe anything until you find how to guide your thoughts."*

(Quote ref. 45) by Buddha. *"We are what we think. All that we are, arises with our thoughts. With our thoughts, we make our world."*

Everything is based on your thoughts. If you think negative thoughts, negativity will be brought to you. If you think positive thoughts, positivity will be brought to you. It's the law of attraction. Like attracts like. If you have a bad attitude, then life looks hard to you. It's all about how you see things.

(Quote ref. 46) by Julio Torri. *"The story of a man 's life dwells in his attitude."*

Always pay attention to your thoughts. Ask yourself, why do I think this and other questions. Everyone talks to themselves all the time. Years ago we were told that's fine, but when you start answering yourself, than you have problems. How insane was that? The saying must have been started by those who didn't want us to think for ourselves. If we got answers, then we might act upon them and then they would call the men in the white coats so they didn't have to deal with us. It was one of those freedom issues again. Let your conscience be your guide is my motto – from Jiminy Cricket.

(Quote ref. 47) by J.B. Phillips. *"Don't let the world squeeze you into its mold."*

(Book ref. 10) *"Flying closer to the Flame"* by Charles Swindoll. "In order for one's conscience to be a good guide – one the spirit can direct – it needs to be healthy- sensitive – and capable of getting God's message and truth."

(Quote ref. 48) by Karl Barth. *"Conscience is the best interpreter of life."*

You make the door. This is your life, but....

Remember how you use to hate (or do hate) assignments at school? In the class of life, you try to find your own assignment. You do this by taking time to yourself and go within to reach your inner self. That what you keep thinking about is what you need to explore first. Your talents are God's gifts to you and what you do with those gifts are your gift to God.

(Quote ref. 49) by Erma Bombeck - *"When I stand before God at the end of my life, I would hope that I would not have a single bit of talent left and I could say, I used everything you gave me."*

You have the chance to put everything together. Use your own mind of how you want to live your life and how you will serve others.

(Quote ref. 50) Elie Wiesel writes: *"Peace is our gift to each other."*

As long as you remain true to yourself and don't hurt anyone intentionally and remember that you can have dreams but that the universe has the final decision – than it will all be good. You have to remember that you can open more doors but have to be aware of what is going on. There are red flags - gut feelings – built in your body to make you stop, look and listen. It's okay to dream and even have a plan, just don't get too attached to the outcome. The outcome and timing belong to God.

(Quote ref. 51) by Penny Peirce *"With intuition, we know what we need to know, right when we need to know it. The universe, it seems, doesn't waste time or energy. Intuition presents information to us when we need it, not a moment too soon or too late, and uses any means available to reach us."*

Divine order - divine order. Say you get fired from your job. Take a step back and see what is ahead for you. If you wallow in your mire, seek revenge and complain over being fired, you won't see the doors of opportunity. You will be spending negative time instead of positive time. If you worry – complain – wallow – than you are just putting yourself back in that unproductive rocking chair again. Vent your feelings to a friend, family member or yourself and God. You will realize that the job was a stepping stone and that it was time to move

44

on. If you really think about it, there was probably something that was not working out on your job or you were thinking of making a change. Since you did not make a change, the universe stepped in and made you change. Everything is connected and done in divine order. Look for new doors to open and be aware of all messages being sent to you. Sometimes things don't make sense at the time but further down the road they will. Always look for the positive and not the negative that a situation is bringing to you.

Maybe your job was draining you in some way. It was meant that you be there for a reason but now it is time to move on to the next lesson. Be in awe as if you are seeing something for the first time. This will put you in a more positive mode. When you have obstacles, figure out the message. Believe me, there is always a message. Usually you are to choose a different path.

(Quote ref. 52) by Marsha Sinetar *"Think of all obstacles as stepping stones to build the life you want."*

(Quote ref. 53) by Harriet Beecher Stowe *"When you get into a tight place and everything goes against you until it seems that you cannot hold on for a minute longer, never give up then, for that is just the place and time when the tide will turn."*

When you say "When I get that promotion", " When I get out of school", "When I'm out on my own," When I have my own car", "When I get my dream home", "When I find a man", " When I find a woman"- you are taking away the journey. You are not enjoying the process – you only want the destination. The problem with this is that when you get these things you will want something else. You will always want more and never savor the present. When you go through something, savor it totally. Live in the present!! Also, tell your loved ones I love you. Say the words to them. Don't wait, because, we don't know what tomorrow brings or even the next moment for that matter.

(Book ref. 11) *"Wouldn't Take Nothing for My Journey Now"* by Maya Angelou– she says; "Life is an ongoing adventure. We leave our homes for work, acting and even believing that we will reach our destinations with no unusual event startling us out of our set expectations. The truth is, we know nothing. Not where our cars will fail or when our buses will stall, whether our places of employment will be there when we arrive, or whether, in fact, we ourselves will arrive whole and alive at the end of our journeys. Life is pure adventure, and the sooner we realize that, the quicker we will be able to treat life as art: to bring all our energies to each encounter, to remain flexible enough to notice and admit when what we expected to happen did not happen. We need to remember that we are created creative and can invent new scenarios as frequently as they are needed."

You make the door but you have to keep your eye on the door and realize that the universe always slips the unexpected in. Keep the door open for any and all possibilities. When you keep the door closed, the universe says (forget this guy). The universe then moves on to the next door that is open for it and you wondered why some people (receive) and you don't. Well now you know!! Be open minded and flexible. Don't be an ingrate. Be grateful for everything. See more under gratitude section.

(Quote ref. 54) by Erica Jong *"And the trouble is, if you don't risk anything, you risk even more."*

Remember, everything has to do with your thoughts. Here are 2 quotes that fit this.

(Quote ref. 55) by Jan Ashford - *"There is no such thing as can't, only won't. If you are qualified, all is takes is a burning desire to accomplish, to make a change. Go forward, go backward. Whatever it takes! But you can't blame other people or society in general. It all comes from your mind. When we do the impossible we realize we are special people."*

(Quote ref. 56) by Henry Ford. *"If you think you can do a thing or think you can't do a thing - you're right."*

You also need to know what to do with what's inside the door or comes out of the door – good and bad. More importantly you need to meditate on what you keep hidden in the door. What are you hiding from and why? Figure out why you are being held back from what you want to do. You need to be constantly aware of that door!!! You need to realize that you are only in control of how you respond to people – things – and that door!

Think of your life as one big puzzle. Pretend you are here to put your own puzzle piece in the big landscape of the world, because, guess what, thats exactly why we're here. We are here to fulfill our assignment. Fit that puzzle piece in where it will serve all and be for the good of all those concerned. We're all connected just like the pieces of a puzzle. The universe has the final decision and it will all be good. Remember: no one can take your thoughts away, so put that thinking cap on and see where you fit in, where you belong. Also, always be sure that faith is constantly in your thoughts. God - the universe - the unexpected and thoughts are your constant companions. Always be ready to expect the unexpected.

(Daily Word ref. 8) "I recognize unexpected events as the out workings of divine order, even if their part in the bigger picture is not yet evident."

(Quote ref. 57) by Lewis Carroll *"There's no use trying Alice said, 'One can't believe impossible things.' 'I dare say you haven't had much practice.' said the Queen, 'When I was your age, I always did it for half-an-hour a day. Why sometimes I've believed as many as six impossible things before breakfast."*

THOUGHTS: Everyday - during your solitude time - ask yourself about your thoughts and feelings. Write them down in *"My Journal Time"*. Are you worried or complaining about something? Why? Ask yourself about patterns that are repeating themselves and if you don't like the patterns – come up with solutions – cut yourself a new path to your journey. Are you living in the present – savoring every moment? Remembering to stop, look and listen? You learned this when you were small. You just need to remember it and apply it again to your life now. Are you doing this? How? Are you seeking a place for your puzzle piece? Where do you think you would serve the world to the best of your knowledge? Have you told your loved ones -I love you? Are you keeping your mind body and soul connected? Are you keeping that door open and being aware of everything? Have you told your self I love you?

47

My Journal

_____

_____

_____

_____

_____

_____

_____

_____

_____

_____

_____

_____

_____

_____

_____

_____

_____

_____

_____

_____

_____

_____

_____

_____

_____

_____

_____

_____

_____

_____

My Journal

My Journal

Chapter 7

Gratitude

You hear people saying "Count your blessings" all the time, but exactly what does that mean and are we truly saying it "Gratefully?" Say thank you and mean it!! One practice that everyone of us (on a daily basis) must do - is be genuinely grateful for everything that has been given to us in this beautiful world we live in. This is hard to do with the things that we think are unfair. I lost my oldest son to an allergy/asthma episode when he was 10 years old. My faith went null at that point and for a long time after. This loss happened back in 1987.

After much reading, I realized that our days really are numbered. Sometimes your assignment is filled and you are sent home. Other assignments are found and filled and take years and years of serving. At one time I had written a childhood girlfriend and said "Did our Danny have to pass away in order for the doctor to realize that *now* he will give all of his allergy patients an Epinephrine Kit?" When my friend Jan wrote back she said, "I'm so sorry about your feelings of loss over Danny. Like you said, others are benefitting over your experience."

This made sense to me. It was like my question was answered. Yes indeed, that was his actual assignment. I could then thank God for, the gift he gave us for 10 years. I'm grateful for the time we had together. We are all here for God's glory. You need to share your experiences in order for God to use them. Use all of your experiences to help others. After I went through the stages of loss, I came across the prayer card that was given out in memory of my son and actually read it and understood it. It started out saying "Mom and Dad, don't cry, that I didn't stay. We all only visit, God planned it that way."

What I will share with you at this moment is that you have to savor every moment and don't take anything for granted. Like I wrote at the beginning of this book, we need to connect mind, body and soul in every waking hour and embrace them like there is no tomorrow – because we are not guaranteed tomorrow. Show and express gratitude and lots of appreciation and tell those that you love, *I love you* often. Don't wait, do it now!!

(Daily Word ref. 9) "Applause, a hug, a smile, any other form of appreciation lifts the spirits of both the one who is giving and the one who is receiving. When we look at others and life itself with gratitude, we are richly rewarded."

Delaying any type of appreciation is not an option!

(Book ref. 12) "*Simple Abundance*" by Sarah Ban Breathnach writes that when awareness arrives you start giving thanks for everything. She writes: "Open the eyes of your eyes. Each day began to offer me authentic moments of pleasure and contentment. But hadn't they before? The difference was that I was now noticing and appreciating each day's gifts. The power of gratefulness caught me by surprise."

Her book contains as she says "An inner journey, a spiritual and practical course in creative living and a tapestry of contentment."

Although this one focuses on women, she also has a book for men.

Going through (not around) lessons reinforces what you have learned. If you are not applying your wisdom of past lessons, than the universe steps in with more lessons. Be aware of everything and be grateful for everything. Stop, look and listen.

Be sure to start a gratitude journal. This is different from "*my journal time*" that you are writing in after each section of this book. Get a notebook that you can enter daily things that you are thankful for. When you first write in it, list everything that you are grateful for up to now. Then, each day thereafter, list what you are grateful for that day. The journal needs to contain things that you don't think of as something to be thankful for. After writing these down you need to write a positive affirmation such as: I understand this is something to be thankful for. When the timing is right I will have an "Ah-ha" moment and say, thats why that happened. If you don't know pain, how will you know when joy and peace arrive?

(Quote ref. 58) by Rabbi Harold Kushner *"If you concentrate on finding whatever is good in every situation, you will discover that your life will suddenly be filled with gratitude, a feeling that nurtures the soul."*

(Book ref. 13) *"The Artists Way: A Spiritual Path to Higher Creativity"* by Julia Cameron she writes "There is a connection between self-nurturing and self-respect."

You need to treat yourself right and this includes being thankful for everything that comes your way. If you avoid what is meaningless to you then you are closing a door to something. Take everything into consideration. Respect the fact that everything is in your life for the highest good of all concerned - even if you don't see it at the time. Grow spiritually and know that you are in partnership with God.

(Quote ref. 59) by Graham Greene: *"Writing is a form of therapy; sometimes I wonder how all those who do not write, compose or paint can manage to escape the madness, the melancholia, the panic and fear which is inherent in a human situation."*

(Quote ref. 60) by Ursula K. Lequin: *"As a writer you are free. You are about the freest person that ever was. Your freedom is what you have bought with your solitude, your loneliness."*

GRATITUDE: *"My Journal Time"*: Have you counted your blessings today? Have you dug deep inside to find your assignment to serve? Will it use you creativity, your talent from above? Have you said thank you for being alive and being able to serve? What are some of the ideas that you came up with? If you took one of these ideas, what can you do today to bring it to a possible occupation? Have you said I'm thankful just to be alive? How did it make you feel? Have you said I love you to your loved ones today and said thank you for being in my life? Don't forget to get your gratitude journal started today which is a daily entry of what you are thankful for. Get a notebook, journal or diary for this.

My Journal

My Journal

My Journal

What you have just read are the three main parts of life: Experiences, thoughts, and gratitude.   Next is a chapter about school and rights. Part two of this book will have entries in ABC order.

Following are two quotes relating to the difference between school and life:

(Quote ref. 61) by Tom Bodett: *"In school you're taught a lesson and than given a test. In life you're given a test that teaches you a lesson."*

(Quote ref. 62) by Soren Kierkegaard: *"Life is a hard teacher; she gives the test first, the lesson after."*

Chapter 8

School / Rights

I knew I was different when my third grade teacher called my parents into school because I used the "wrong" word. We were in the classroom and were shown cards. We were asked to look at 3 words given and then put down a word that describes all of them (put them in a category-put one label on them). I remember this like it was yesterday. The words were: shirt, dress, coat. The "correct word", the word they wanted was, clothes. Everyone wrote down clothes except nonconformist Nancy, I put down "garment". I also wanted to put down apparel and attire but didn't know if there were 2 p's and 2 t's and I didn't want those dreaded red x marks. I got a red mark anyway and a note for my parents.

My parents were called in because I used a word that was inappropriate for a 9 year old. The teacher asked if that is the word they use for clothes. They said yes. She told them to use the word clothes from now on and to use "easier" words at home. Can you imagine that? Stifled at 9 years old and not being able to learn something outside the school building. How insane is that?

Definition Of School:

An educational establishment. United group or sect. A specific method. (School board)- A body governing local schools. (Govern) – Rule with authority – guide – control. (sect) – religious denomination.

Problem :

Schools teach a specific method. If someone learns in a different way, heavens to Betsey they are labeled abnormal. They feel they have lost control if you are a little different.

(Quote ref. 63) Jodie Foster: *"Normal is not something to aspire to, it's something to get away from."*

Schools are a sect in themselves. That's why they don't want religion in the school. Actually, I agree, it shouldn't be taught in the school. I personally believe that spirituality is the "universal window" and that we all need to learn and generate kindness, love, understanding, peace and integrity to all, regardless of what our religious denomination is. Spirituality should be taught from early on both at school and at home. We are considered robots. We are taught to do things a certain way. Here's a formula, now memorize it. The memorizer gets a high grade and the non memorizer gets a low grade. This will of course put a negative factor into the child's brain and he/she will eventually become bored with school. They are shot down/stifled before they even get started on their journey. They try to do what is expected of them but eventually say "whats the use?" It's sad to think how many minds have been stifled from not being able to use Gods' given gifts. No one can make any progress when they are put on an unproductive path. When we are (young) we do not realize that we need to look these "naysayers" in the face and say – I will become stronger because of this experience. As we grow, we need to be aware that we can and should grow from each and every experience. It's important to remember to always look for the positive in all situations. Don't slump back and give – in and become unproductive. See what you can learn from the "naysayers" and move on from there.

If someone is bullying you in some way, maybe they have old wounds to open up and heal. You just got in the crossfire of their wound. I have found that talking to people and asking about their life, gives you clues to why they are the way they are. People are not a certain way for no reason. Finding the reasons breaks the barriers and than the healing can begin. Even if they are not ready to heal, at least you will be able to have a different reaction to their behavior.

(Quote ref. 64) by Alice Walker: *"No person is your friend who demands your silence, or denies your right to grow."*

The educational system is no ones friend. If you're an educator, speak up and make a difference for the good of all. There are changes to be made and each and everyone of us can make a difference. Here's a quote that fits well here.

(Quote ref. 65) by Bob Proctor: *"No amount of reading or memorizing will make you successful in life. It is the understanding and application of wise thought which counts."*

Use what you have learned. Your wisdom is a tool that should be used to be for the good of all concerned. It's boring sitting and memorizing things such as long division a million times or taking Algebra for a whole semester. What kind of motivation is that? Teach how to explore thoughts. How to express feelings and find creative talents. We're not in school to fill in time of the school day with unproductive repetition. There is no such thing as ADD. Attention Deficit Disorder is just a label put on someone who isn't cooperating as the cog that the so called educators expect them to be. If someone learns in a different way, then teach them in a different way!! What the H-E double hockey sticks do you think we are all here for ?? Isn't it to help each other?? Stop putting on labels. Ask what people are feeling.

(Book ref. 14) *"In their own way"* by Thomas Armstrong writes "If your child sticks out one iota from the norm – in other words, if your child shows his true individual nature – then there is always the danger that he will be discriminated against or stuck with some sort of label and treated like a category instead of a real human being."

It's your life. Don't give in. Look from within. Human beings are treated like cogs on a wheel. As long as we do everything the same- keep their machine running- we are "normal". What if the person who defined "normal" was "abnormal". Just something to think about.

Human beings are here for a specific assignment from above and if we all remain a cog then we will not be able to use our creativity and talents. Every single thing in the world has first been an idea from someones mind. Schools are just starting to have fundings for the arts. This is because the arts give us choices and allow us to use our creativity and that means individuality will surface and thats something schools do not want. It's too hard to control us when we have minds of our own.

In school we are graded for using our memory basically. We are also graded for doing something the "normal" way. This does nothing for us in the way of preparing us for life after school. Life does not have a standard formula. No wonder so many get lost in life. That's all we grow up with is formulas. We graduate and then we're told to go out in the world and live. If we don't have good memories and only learned one way of doing everything, then we are back to that cog again and won't be able to use our true talents that we were sent here to use. Be a cog on your own machine. Have your mind, body and soul work together. Than you can say "oh what a cog I am" instead of being a cog on "their" machine which very seldom works toward being a positive running machine. We all do have a voice to change that however.

We mess up somewhere along the line and we're told; you're an adult now, deal with it. No one told us that in order to live in the world that we would have to learn lessons by actually experiencing a million and one different scenarios and that the outcomes are based on our own attitudes /choices and not formulas given to us and then ultimately changed by the universe. The universe always has the last word - be buddies with it. The universe is a lifetime buddy!!!

Parents blame the schools, schools blame the parents. Wake up people. We are not back in the Garden Of Eden. Communication and coming to mutual agreements are extremely lacking in the world. Understanding and kindness need to be put into practice both individually and globally.

(Quote ref. 66) by John F. Kennedy: *"Our task... is not to fix blame for the past, but to fix the course for the future."*

Solutions And Rights

We need to be able to be ourselves and of course within reason, be able to use different ways of communicating. If someone uses the word garment instead of what the school has for the "right" answer, then I don't think they should warrant getting a red mark. The answer is correct.

My youngest son Jake was born in September. When he turned five we were sent a letter stating that any child born between September and December could be tested and placed in school that year and not wait until the next year. He took the test and had 1 answer wrong . The teacher said it wasn't really "wrong" but that it wasn't the answer they were looking for. I'm like, this is deja vu. Jake was asked which way water falls. His answer was *south*. They were looking for the word *down* but since *south* is down they gave it to him as a right answer. I was happy to see that the schools have come a long way since my days there but they still have room for improvement.

We all need to persevere the issue of funding for the arts. We could even go as far as going back to the way it was years ago and in other countries. We should go to 8th grade and learn the basics and then 9th through 12th grade we should be in an apprentice type program in school. Have classes that pertain only to what we think we may want to get into as an adult. We need to be able to use our talent/ creativity.

(Quote ref. 67) by Anna Freud: *"Creative minds have always been known to survive any kind of bad training."*

The Montessori method of education promotes creativity, independence of thought and action, a positive self image, joy, and a spirit of service to others and the world. Creativity needs to be acknowledged more fully in the schools.

(Daily Word ref. 10) "We don't know all we can do until we give ourselves permission to be creative – to sing, dance, paint, write, or do whatever our creative spirit leads us in doing."

Schools need to set time aside to allow students to reach fully into their creative minds. We are not robots. When your creative energy is locked up you become stressed and bored. This then goes to various unproductive outlets – one being - the bully and onto crime. Kids become bullies when they can't express themselves in more appropriate ways. When they can't find their talents, they pick on others. Their unproductive outlets, in turn, makes others become unproductive because they are being picked on. So round and round it goes like a domino effect.

These last 4 years should also include scenarios for real life experiences with role playing. It sure makes a lot more sense to role play at this age rather than go crazy later on in life. Cause and effect should be emphasized more and it should be stressed more that we should go within to find our feelings, thoughts, talents and attitudes on issues.

More importantly we should be able to express our feelings, thoughts, talents and attitudes. This falls under wisdom. It doesn't do any good just to know what we feel inside. We also need to be able to express those feelings in everyday life. We are all unique and are here to complete an assignment. In order to do that we need to be able to express ourselves in every way, shape and form.

The Declaration of Independence - "We hold these truths to be self-evident, that all men are created equal, that they are endowed by their Creator with certain unalienable rights that among these are life, liberty and the pursuit of happiness."

I believe that Thomas Jefferson is turning over in his grave because of the way we are living his strong beliefs in the rights of man and a government derived by the people. Anyone reading this is alive so you have life. There are of course issues such as capital punishment and abortion. Now lets explore liberty and the pursuit of happiness. Liberty is defined as: freedom from bondage, captivity, restraint, etc. The pursuit of happiness is where we get messed up. We are not guaranteed happiness – we need to pursue it. Pursue is defined as: Follow with intent to catch. Continue to seek after, be engaged in. Pursuit is to carry out an occupation. Happiness is to be glad, joyous, satisfied, agreeable and unworried.

The way I see it, we are restrained in school and it doesn't get much better after that. As long as we continue to put the matter of our happiness in the hands of others, our pursuing will be unproductive. It is our assignment – our occupation – to find out what we intend to catch – or attract. Everything we do should be carried out with the intention of making our world a better place. We all need to work together and not allow just a hand full of people to make decisions. In order for happiness and peace we need to come to agreements – not fight!!!

(Daily Word ref. 11) "Today I ready myself to live the life of abundance that is God's will for me. It is a life filled with joy, a life of peace."

The United States is so mixed up that we fight amongst ourselves. What's with being a Democrat or Republican? The debates are totally senseless as is the money that is being spent for the campaigning. They bring up health costs, social security, poverty etc. and all the while they are spending thousands and millions of dollars going around and making us believe they will be the one to make a difference. Well, their making a difference alright. The difference between giving the money to the country and giving it to themselves. All campaign expenses are a waste and should be used for health costs, social security, poverty etc. Now that would be making a difference!!

No one said it would be easy for the United States to try and have peace with all different ethnic/race backgrounds and religions. Most other nations – the people have basically the same backgrounds. It sometimes seems, however, that we are using this as an experiment – to see if we can do this. We seem to be in the destruction business instead of the construction business. We should be of the people, by the people and for the people.

(Lyrics ref. 18) *"Fly like an eagle"* - "Feed the babies – who don't have enough to eat. Shoe the children – with no shoes on their feet. House the people – livin in the street. Oh, Oh there's a solution."

(Bible ref. 10) Luke: 3:11 "Whoever has two coats must share with anyone who has none; and whoever has food must do likewise."

We are also told that we have rights in the preamble of the constitution. It starts out "We the people of the United States." We the people - repeat – we the people!

It doesn't say, We the president, We the senator, We the governor, etc. (Wake up people) we are the people – and the only say so that We have - is to vote. Big deal. That doesn't get us anywhere. They let us choose someone in an election. Big wow!! Now what?? We were pacified and given the right to vote and we settled for that. Helloooooo people. Are all your lights completely out? Is anyone home upstairs? To vote is the limit of our rights and freedom. Nothing else is derived by the people.

We are restrained and controlled - there is no freedom. I'm sorry but I don't hear our freedom bell ringing!! Let freedom ring? Tell me

64

where? I don't hear it. Either I'm deaf or I'm not in Kansas anymore or any other part of the United States for that matter.

The only place I heard the freedom bell ringing was at Disney inside Liberty Square and we all know - that's just a hop, skip and a jump from Fantasy Land!!

(Daily Word ref. 12) "True freedom is freedom from limitation – whether external or internal, whether prolonged or brief. I am free to choose new paths toward ever-changing horizons in my celebration of life."

To celebrate life you need to feel good and you need to be able to demonstrate and express those feelings.

In 2006 I received a birthday card from my brother in-law Gary. It was from Blue Mountain E-cards. It's called: *A Celebration of You* "This is a celebration of the day you were born and all the days that have passed between then and now that have made you who you are today. This is a celebration of every song that plays inside your heart, and all the ways you've touched and blessed our world with your story. This is your day to shine! Happy birthday." Thanks Gary – god bless you! It truly came at the utmost time that I needed a little boost. We are here to live and celebrate life, not be limited.

We tell our kids to get along and be agreeable. Come to terms so that outcomes are for the good of all concerned and then they are bombarded in the streets, bombarded with the media sensationalism and bombed in war. We are giving them a double standard- do as I say – not as I do.

I remember one history class test that had us memorize 50 various dates and matching war hero's names and/or events. Civil War dates, World War dates, and other such events only serve the purpose of impressing upon us that we never learn from our lessons. What happened to WW1 being the war to end all wars? I guess it was just something to add to the history books-something to just reminisce about on what should have been.

(Quote ref. 68) by Margaret Mead: *"We need to devise a system within which peace will be more rewarding than war."*

(Lyrics ref.19). *"War"* - "War – huh - what is it good for - absolutely nothing. Say it again!! Oh no – there's got to be a better way."

And, how does war have anything to do with brotherhood?

(Lyrics ref. 20) *"America the beautiful"* - "America, America - God shed His grace on thee - and crown thy good in brotherhood from sea to shining sea."

What did we do, learn these songs and not be *aware* of the words?

(Quote ref. 69)   by Jeannette Rankin: *"We have to get it into our heads once and for all that we cannot settle disputes by eliminating human beings."*

I don't need to boggle my brain with war dates. We all need to get together, be united and stop being hypocrites. America is totally unproductive. If knowing such useless information as dates turns you on or you want to be on Jeopardy or win trivia games, then do all this memorizing during 9th -12th stint or your own time. This falls under one mans trash is another mans treasure. Certain so called valuable information should not be part of schoolings curriculum. Some of us don't need to learn dates on a routine basis. There is no rhyme or reason for it.

Also , the grading system should be changed to (U) for understands and (NH) for needs help. More essays should be written than true/ false questions which remind me of Russian roulette.   Seriously, we shouldn't be graded purely on memorizing or 50/50 luck. If you want to have matching on tests, match inventors and people who brought positive results into the world – learn what they did - and not dates of disasters that we never learned a damn thing from.

It always has amazed me that humans call themselves the intelligent ones on this planet, because if you really think about it, it takes us the longest to learn how to do things. Animals eat by instinct and some walk soon after birth. Things come very natural at a young age to our nature critters and animals. We could learn from ants - they all work together. They go about their business and never do any complaining. You don't see or hear them disagreeing. They know what they have to do and they just do it.

(Book ref. 15) The story of *"The Ants and the Grasshopper"* – from Aesop's Fables - The grasshopper played around all summer - not putting away food - while the ants worked hard putting food away for the winter. The grasshopper didn't survive. Moral of the story – the productive ants survived – because they all worked together and didn't disagree. Smart little critters. No wonder those fire ants bite us. They're trying to light a fire under our butts so we will be more productive like they are. And another thing to think about. If you want to do something to better the world but think no one will listen to little you, then read this:

(Quote ref. 7) by Anita Roddick: *"If you think you're too small to have an impact, try going to bed with a mosquito in the room."*

If those little buggers can get our attention, than certainly we can accomplish something somewhere out in the world.

(Quote ref. 71) by Albert Einstein: *"The intellect has little to do on the road to discovery. There comes a leap in consciousness, call it intuition or what you will, and the solution comes to you, and you don't know how or why."*

(Quote ref. 72) by Albert Einstein: *"We never cease to stand like curious children before the great mystery into which we were born."*

Wake up people. We learned the basics before we were 5 and some more in kindergarten. Learn to understand, love and get along. What is it that we fear? Why does our ego get in the way? By the way ego stands for: Easing God Out.

This is from a poem:

(Quote ref. 73) "The Invitation" by Oriah Mountain Dreamer: *"It doesn't interest me where or what or with whom you have studied. I want to know what sustains you, from the inside, when all else falls away."* It can be read in it's entirety at www.sapphyr.net. *(Pearls of Wisdom Quotes– Native American Wisdom).*

SCHOOL/RIGHTS: *"My Journal Time"* – write down what you think about the process of learning. Agree – or disagree with me? Why?

What are some ways in which you think your ideas might benefit the world? Speak up and let your voice be heard – anyone can make a difference. You don't want those ants to overcome us like they do in those sci-fi movies do you? Then get out there and make a difference!! Get out there and be productive!! Get out there and kick ass.

(Quote ref. 74)   by Maya Angelou: *"I love to see a young girl go out and grab the world by the lapels. Life's a bitch -you've got to go out and kick ass."*

My Journal

My Journal

My Journal

PART TWO

Chapter 9

Adventure

While driving back to Orlando on I-4 from Cassadaga, Florida – one day in May 2004, I could hardly wait to get home and retrieve my box full of 40 years research. I knew I wanted to write since I was 9 years old. I collected affirmations, quotations, ideas, stories, my thoughts on life - some on little scraps of papers or napkins that I could hardly read anymore. Some were in old books in the margins. I started collecting in a pencil box – then graduated to a shoe box and now have it all in a 20 gallon plastic container.

How on earth did that medium healer in Cassadaga know about my hidden box full of my special inspirational goodies. Well dah, Nancy-shes a psychic. She had said to me "You have wonderful ideas that you have in a box, look at them, now is the time to write. It doesn't have to be a dream anymore, put away in a closet. Take time for yourself now, make it enjoyable, and yeah, go for it."

Not everyone believes in psychics, if you don't, just be a little open minded here. Never assume a damn thing. Don't close doors – or even windows for that matter. I stopped off at Wal -mart and bought some notebooks, tape and pens. I needed to organize everything. I know I had a wide grin on my face that would probably put the smiley Cheshire Cat (The cat that Alice – from Alice in Wonderland came across) to shame. Just then I realized I would not have that much time to devote to write now. At the time I was working for Disney. In February of 2000, I had made it out with myself that I would work at Disney at least 5 years. You learn a lot about people from all over the world and that we all are extremely unique, yet the same. I had a lot of fun going to all the parks but the thing that I cherish the most, is that I was told by cast members and guests, that I made a difference in their life. It had become a very rewarding experience in that respect. I was once again surprised by the universe and it's divine order and lessons. I gave, but more importantly, received blessings.

When I got home I got my 20 gallon box out. As I opened the lid, numerous thoughts came flowing over me. More then numerous, abundant thought, joyous wellspring of thoughts, an ocean of thoughts. I started to cry, happy tears of joy. Immediately I was drawn to a poster I have called Ecstasy – by Maxfield Parrish. In the picture is a young girl in her 20's standing on a mountain with her arms holding her neck and holding up her gorgeous curly long locks of hair. She has a fabulous smile on her face and has her head held high looking up – out at the sky and mountain tops. You can almost hear her say: I will climb every mountain!!!

It seems fitting to me to mention this song at this point.

(Lyrics ref. 21) *"Climb every Mountain"* - "Climb every mountain – search high and low. A *dream* that will need all the love you can give – everyday of your life – for as long as you live. The hills are alive with the sound of music - my heart wants to sing every song it hears."

(Quote ref. 75) by Lin-Chi: *"Thinking brings us to the foot of the mountain; faith brings us to the top."*

The first thought that I had was that it took me 40 years to collect this stuff (some of it just my opinions) and that I enjoyed collecting it, even though I didn't exactly know what I was going to do with it all. So, I guess you could say that I enjoyed and savored that time of preparation, enjoyed the journey, not really knowing what the destination would be. I went with the flow and let go, and let God.

(Bible ref. 11) In Ecclesiastes:3 we are told " To everything there is a season, A time for every purpose under heaven."

Had I started the book after 10 years of collecting, I wouldn't have had the silly things my kids said and did, I wouldn't have had the experiences to share with others. It was an adventure just finding everything and experiencing it, even though I didn't know exactly what I was going to do with it all. I can now say I went through (the experiences) in order to share with others. Always remember life is not about the destination – it's about the journey.

I maybe didn't have time to devote fully to writing but I did have days off to gather everything together and organize it. The present moment would be used to (remember everything and prepare) for when I would have total time to devote to my book.

If Alice wouldn't have been curious and fallen into the rabbit hole, there would have been no Adventure in Wonderland. I grew up with Rabbit, The Mad Hatter and the Cheshire Cats' silly grin, not to forget Dee and Dum, The Queen of Hearts and all the other unique characters Alice met on her curious adventurous journey.

If the witch in The Wizard of Oz wouldn't have been a snake in the grass, Dorothy would have stayed home with Toto and then Dorothy wouldn't have been knocked silly on her noggin and dreamt her adventure. She would have been safe and sound in the storm cellar and not dreamt at all. Many of us wouldn't have been reminded that we need to learn to use our brain-learn (Scarecrow) , have courage-risk (Lion) or have a heart-love (Tin Man). Dorothy said; "Theres no place like home." Sometimes you have to leave home to find things out.

Let's take The Wizard of Oz one step farther. Dorothy knew that she had to go see the wizard. She knew she had to follow the yellow brick road to get there. When she got to the forest, she knew she had to go through it, but what she didn't know is what she would find in the forest, the details were unknown, the universe (God) is in the details!! You can follow your path (your yellow brick road) but know that surprises may force you to pick a new path – that often will serve your true self better.

(Quote ref. 76) Glinda the Good Witch said: *"Your power was with you all along."*

You don't have to look farther than yourself – but sometimes you have to cut a new path to find that out.

(Daily Word ref. 13) "I am flexible. I have the courage and faith to explore new paths to greater possibilities."

It's okay to go out on a limb and find out what your assignment is – just remember all you have learned and apply it to everyday life, otherwise your experiences are all for naught. We venture out to see where we belong in the world.

(Lyrics ref. 22) *"Colors of the Wind"* - "You'll learn things you never knew you never knew...We need to sing with all the voices of the mountain – We need to paint with all the colors of the wind."

Making changes and growing is the only way that you are really living – anything else is being in a stagnant not getting anywhere situation. Being in any type of pain either mentally or physically is always a sign to make a change. Don't be shot down – whatever the pain – grow stronger from it.

(Quote ref. 77) by Amado Nervo: *"Evolution moves from unconsciousness to ecstasy through pain."*

If you need to go out on a journey for awhile – do so – leave your comfort zone. Learn all you can and when you feel you have accomplished what you were looking for – then go to what will serve you and be for the good of all concerned. I will end this section with saying, make an adventure of life. Find out your assignment in life by going within and doing what speaks to you, your inner voice.

(Quote ref. 78) Like Brian Tracy says: *"Decide upon your major definite purpose in life and then organize your activities around it."*

(Quote ref. 79) Jiminy Cricket: *"When your heart is in your dream, no request is too extreme."* From Pinocchio.

Your adventure – the making of you: Instructions included but assembly is required by you. No two will be alike. You will be an original with only one thing in common with others. You will all be creatures of loving yourselves and others. On the journey-transformation is urged. Don't fight change. Work with it and go through the changes-never around the changes. You will be in a state of awe with all the surprises that the universe has to offer. Be like Dorothy and get knocked on the head by windows and doors a few times and soon your life will have windows and doors that open up to beautiful changes. Your true colors will come out and show you what you are really made of.

ADVENTURE: *"My Journal Time"* – What do you do that's adventurous? Make a list of things you want to learn – go outside your comfort zone and pursue your purpose. Are you listening to your inner voice? How? Can you do some things that are connected to that voice that might lead you to your purpose? Write down your plan-but leave room for the unexpected.

My Journal

My Journal

My Journal

Chapter 10

Assume

(Book ref. 16) In the book "*The Four Agreements*" by Don Miguel Ruiz - he lists the agreements as : " Be Impeccable With Your Word, Don't Take Anything Personally, Don't Make Assumptions, and Always Do Your Best."

My sister-in- law Eileen told me about this book – Thanks Eileen. I am now taking this opportunity to recommend it to all of you.

Making assumptions causes misunderstandings. Always ask questions and see things as clearly as possible. When someone talks to you or they write a letter – try to find out exactly what they are saying – don't take words out of context – and make your own story based on what you assume that you have heard or read. Don't assume what you see either. Assuming is highly unproductive.

Many times people are with someone who plays games of who they are in order to keep peace. This can be highly unproductive when someone gives in and is boiling on the inside. Nothing but built up resentment and anger can be accomplished when assuming that you can make someone happy by giving in. This is putting up a front and can cause nothing but frustration for all people involved.

ASSUME: *"My Journal Time"* – Make a list of things you are not sure of. Try to get the answers to anything that is unclear. Communicate with everyone in a way that there will be less misunderstandings. If you can't talk with someone about something – then try writing a letter to them. Are you afraid to rock the boat on an issue with someone? If your answer was yes – you need to nip the situation in the bud – go through what it takes to make the situation better instead of going around it - which is always unproductive. Rock that boat!

My Journal

My Journal

My Journal

Chapter 11

Attachment

It is extremely important to find yourself first before finding someone to go through life with. Many believe that we have to find someone in order to be complete. Why is it that so many of us feel we can not be complete and whole alone?

(Book ref. 17) *"Return to Love"* - Marianne Williamson. "Under the holy spirits guidance we come together to share joy. Under the egos direction we come together to share our desperation."

When we are complete as ourselves, then and only then will we attract the right people and things in our lives for us. You want to come together and have joy - not be desperate and needy for each other.

(Quote ref. 80) by Jean-Paul Sartre: *"Life begins on the other side of desperation."*

A real problem comes about when you assume an attachment. This is where you assume that someone is wonderful and every waking hour is consumed with them. When they fall off the pedestal that you put them on, they are the bad guy. Say what? Yes its true – people do that.

(Book ref. 9) *"Why your life sucks"* by Alan H. Cohen. "When they discover you are not who they thought you were or they cannot have you, out come the spears...refuse to accept goo-goo eyed adoration, which always comes with a price tag."

Alan also has a section on; Your Possessions Possess You. Many people get so attached to their possessions that the possessions become more important then themselves. Alan writes, "But many people are owned by their stuff more than they own it. They hassle to get it, sweat to pay it off, spend a lot of time keeping it intact, worry about others marring it, fight over who gets it in the divorce or will, and resists its ultimate demise. Your stuff can drive you crazy." " Have all the stuff you want as long as you are enjoying it. If it starts to run your life, either get rid of it or get rid of your attachment to it."

Since I'm on the subject of possessions I have a few words on hoarding. We can only wear so much, I mean really people, two weeks worth of clothes is enough. How many dishes do you need? How many nick knacks do you need? How much sports equipment do you need? How much of a collection is enough? Hoarding means you don't trust that God will always provide. If you are saving for some day and hoarding for the future – you are going against the rule of living for today. Pray more and want less. Hoarding falls into the worry mode, which is unproductive.

Being a pack rat is saying to others that you are angry and hurt about something or someone has taken something from you. In return, you are going to hold on to everything and anything, even if you have to pay out money to store it or live in a maze. Holding on to stuff will not ease your hurt. Forgiving and moving on is the only way to heal. Having things cannot heal. Hoarding is a form of denial, not having faith and refusal to forgive.

When your life is guided by your spiritual purpose and money and possessions become more then you need, you will know what you need to do, you will share.

(Bible quote ref. 12) Luke 11:3 "Give us day by day our daily bread."

Meaning live one day at a time. Day by day – you will be given what you truly need.

(Book ref. 12) by Sarah Ban Breathnach "Today I would love for all of us to get it at last: not to focus on what we don't have, but to be grateful for what we do. For us to accept, give thanks, bless, and share. For us not to hoard or hold back for fear that there won't be enough. Because Spirit lacks for nothing. As long as you have a few loaves and fishes, and know what to do with them, all you have is all you need."

(Bible quote ref. 13)   Luke 12:15 "Take heed and beware of coveting, for one's life does not consist in the abundance of the things he possesses."

(Quote ref. 81) by Will Rogers: *"Too many people spend money they haven't earned, to buy things they don't want, to impress people they don't like."*

(Quote ref. 82)   Tibetan quote: *"Not with what we have, but with what we enjoy, do we find our true abundance."*

When you lose the stuff, you gain yourself. When you don't have so much to contend to – you become more content.

ATTACHMENT: *"My Journal Time"* – How do you feel about materialism? Do you have a lot of clutter that is being held on to for SOMEDAY? Make a choice of what you are going to do with something and do it NOW. If you have collections – do you still enjoy them or have you outgrown them? Do you buy things to impress others or do you enjoy what you have? Do you feel complete when you are by yourself – or do you constantly need someone around or lots of things around?

My Journal

My Journal

My Journal

Chapter 12

Awareness

(Quote ref. 83) "The Awakening" and is written by Sonny Carroll.

These are just key points – not written in its entirety. It can be found in it's entirety at www.sapphyr.net.

"A time comes in your life when you finally get it. You begin to accept people as they are. Peace and contentment is born of forgiveness. You learn to open up to new worlds and different points of view. There is power and glory in creating and contributing. You learn that alone does not mean lonely. You come to realization that you deserve to be treated with love, kindness, sensitivity and respect and you won't settle for less. You learn that your body really is your temple. And you begin to care for it and treat it with respect. You learn that in order to achieve success you need direction, discipline and perseverance. You also learn that no one can do it all alone... and that it's OK to risk asking for help. You learn to be thankful and to take comfort in many of the simple things we take for granted. Finally, with courage in your heart and God by your side you take a stand, you take a deep breath, and you begin to design the life you want to live as best you can."

Whenever you feel that funky feeling (think there is a lyric here too) coming on that something isn't quite right, stop, look and listen. Mind, body, and soul are always connected. It's a message to you to try and see things differently.

(Lyrics ref. 23) *"A Whole New World"* in the movie Aladdin: "A new fantastic point of view. A hundred thousand things to see. Every turn a surprise. With new horizons to pursue."

(Bible ref. 14) Isaiah 43:19 "Behold, I will do a new thing – Now it shall spring forth – shall you not know it?"

AWARENESS is best learned during your solitude time when you have the time to be totally into your thoughts and your environment. It is a disciplined learning process that can only be fully appreciated by your attitude and your compassion. It co-exists with wisdom because you have to put all of your experiences into action in order to benefit the rewards.

AWARENESS: *"My Journal Time"* – Make an effort to be aware of everything at school, home, work, or out and about today. Also take notice of what you do for yourself. Then - when you come home and write in your journal - write down what you observed. Did you notice things that you never did before? Were you surprised at how people treat one another? Did you notice people sharing love, kindness, respect for one another or the opposite? How did you treat yourself today? Did you feed your MIND BODY AND SOUL in every way shape and form? How did you treat others? What were the blessings you received today?

My Journal

My Journal

My Journal

Chapter 13

Body

Your body is a sacred vessel that should be treated with the utmost care. Your thoughts feed your body as much, if not more, than food. Your body responds to everything that you think.

(Book ref. 6) *"You can heal your life"* by Louise L. Hay – she says: "I believe we create every so-called illness in our body. The body, like everything else in life, is a mirror of our inner thoughts and beliefs. The body is always talking to us, if we will only take the time to listen."

I use to get the flu around my birthday for many years. After living in Wisconsin for my first 43 years of life before moving to Florida, I began thinking of this flu business and my birthday month, December. It's a hectic month but even more so, its cold. The change in temperature and the holidays can play havoc with your body.

I read something one time about saying a statement and making it come true. I realized that for many years I would say "I always get the flu around my birthday." As soon as I realized that saying those words made it so (law of attraction) I changed to saying "I love myself - my mind, body and soul are working in harmony to stay healthy." I thought it was silly but it worked. Sure I might get the flu but now I'm not inviting it at a certain time.

Shortly after this awakening is when I came across *"You can heal your life"* by Louise L. Hay (Book ref. 6) and every time I have a physical problem I look at the list in the book and see what my mind is telling my body. Nine times out of ten I hear myself saying "Oh my God" because it coincides with something I am going through at the time.

Here is an example of how it works: I have never had a cold sore. Then one day I got one. I looked up (cold sore) in Louise Hays book. It says "Festering angry words and fear of expressing them."

The affirmation to this is "I only create peaceful experiences because I love myself. All is well." When you read the next section (Being) you will see what happened shortly after this. Note: This also brought my attention to the divine order of everything.

(Quote ref. 84) Erica Jong writes: *"The body is wiser than its inhabitants. The body is the soul. We ignore its aches, its pains, its eruptions, because we fear the truth. The body is God's messenger."*

You are what you eat and you are what eats you. Once again mind, body and soul unite. At this point I want to mention what negativity can do to your mind, body and soul. There are a lot of toxic people around. They are part of the weeding out that I mentioned earlier. Sometimes you just have to be kind to yourself and weed out people that are not treating you the way you deserve to be treated. Talk to them and if you can't come to an agreement of terms, then say bye and God bless. Your mind, body and soul deserve to be around positive thoughts and uplifting situations. When you are dragged down by someone, your mind, body and soul will suffer.

(Daily Word ref. 14) "I deserve to live in an environment that encourages relaxation and renewal as well as peaceful productivity."

If you tell someone your visions and dreams and they have negative remarks for everything you say, then say bye to those naysayers.

(Quote ref. 85) Wyland (World renowed marine artist) says this: *"There are two types of people: anchors and motors. You want to lose the anchors and get with the motors, because the motors are going somewhere and they're having more fun. The anchors will just drag you down."*

(Book ref. 18) *"Sacred Pampering Principles"* by Debra Jackson Gandy "Every thought and emotion we experience causes a chemical response in our bloodstream, our organs, and our immune system. Negative thoughts create kinks in the continuous flow of the body's chi energy (continuous body's vital life force). Cancer is caused by "deep resentment" held for a long time until it literally eats away at the body."

Again mind, body and soul connect.

(Book ref. 19) "*Creative Visualization*" by Shakti Gawain "I am vibrantly healthy and radiantly beautiful." "I am open to receiving all the blessings of this abundant universe." "I give thanks for divine restoration in mind, body and financial affairs, and in all my relationships now." "I am now attracting loving satisfying relationships into my life." "I am always in the right place at the right time, successfully engaged in the right activity." "Everything I need is coming to me easily and effortlessly." "Everything I need is already within me." "I am one with great spirit."

BODY: "*My Journal Time*" – What did you do for your sacred vessel today? How did you listen to your body today? Is it crying out to you and letting you know something needs to be changed? Is everyone in your life a positive force for you? If not – what can you do to change the situation? How did you feed your mind, body and soul today? If you are with people that drag you down – are you able to see the message that they are presenting to you? Have you let your boundaries down? What can you do to make this negative situation a positive one?

My Journal

My Journal

My Journal

Chapter 14

Being

We are human beings not human doings. So many people are running on automatic pilot these days that it seems that everything is in perpetual motion. Be comes first, then Do, just like in the dictionary. Restoring yourself daily is not an option. You must do this to connect with your mind, body and soul.

You need to sleep, and nap, there is a difference. Sleeping is for recharging and nourishing your body. It requires 6-8 hours to do this. Napping is caring for your mind and soul. You need to do this at least once a day for at least half an hour. If you are at work, take one of your breaks to just put your head down and relax. You're not being anti-social. You're silencing yourself so that you can be refreshed and ready to take on what comes up next. Getting burnt out won't serve you or anyone else.

(Bible ref. 15) Psalm 23:1-3 "The Lord is my shepherd, I shall not want. He makes me lie down in green pastures; he leads me beside still waters; he restores my soul."

Always just sit and be first before you become a doer.

If you would actually sit down and just be, you could possibly see an obstacle or a red flag message sooner. Then you could deal with it before it got out of hand. Obstacles are a good thing, but if you can catch it before manifesting into something big, you will recover easier. You will also see what it is trying to teach you in a more clear way. You will have less suffering and get on with life. Also, like I wrote in my temptation section about Marianne Williamsons quote, I just have to write it here again :"We suffer according to the level of our bullshit." We need to stop the bullshit.

I got caught up in perpetual motion in 2001. Everything became bullshit! I had a crash course. Everything was in perpetual motion. God was telling me what I needed to do but I wasn't listening. He knew though that I could handle it all at once. I was the wounded skin. God was my bandage ripper. I needed to heal old wounds , so God took the bandage off all at once. Ouch! Ouch! Ouch! Wounds need to be healed in open air, not closed up! As I look back now, one big Ouch at the same time was the best way. Quickly rip off the bandage and deal with the pain all at once so that you can start the healing process. If you hide the hurts under a bandage by closing up, then you will never heal.

It was one of those times where you can't see what is really going on, so the universe steps in and changes the motion and gives you time to stop, look and listen. You learn what you have to learn. He starts up a different motion so that you can be and see. That's why it's so important to always be aware!

(Quote ref. 86) "*Tale of Two Cities*" by Charles Dickens "*It was the best of times, it was the worst of times. It was the age of wisdom, it was the age of foolishness.*"

My husband and I had just bought a house in Orlando. Our daughter and son were graduated from high school and both had jobs they enjoyed. A lot of old wounds had been built up basically between all 4 of us. One day in March of 2001, my husband and I got in a heated argument and I told him to leave. When I got home from work he had moved his clothes out. We were on a totally angry unproductive path and were basically in perpetual motion and doing and not being. Twenty-five years had gone by and then I realized I said things would get better *when*. I even realized that my husband use to say "Things will be better when I retire from my job." He retired from that job in 1995 and basically I didn't see any changes in our relationship in these last 6 years. I said " It's not a job or anything else – it's us." The universe stepped in so that we had to make a change.

Both my son and daughter said that we were both much better people on our own than we were as a couple.

(Bible ref. 16) Matthew 11:28 "Come to me, all you who labor and are heavy laden, and I will give you rest."

We all had our peaceful time that Louise Hay was talking about in her affirmation stated above. We all had a chance to look back to reflect and spend solitude time to delete and weed some issues out alone. Then, when the timing was right we could start talking about our future relationships meaning all 4 of us and communicate more effectively.

By having peaceful time we could all go through the stages that we needed to. Had anger gotten worse for any one of us, it could have gone on to a serious illness. One of us could have gotten cancer which Louise Hay describes in her book as: "Deep hurt and/or deep resentment held for a long time until it literally eats away at the body." She also says "Learning to love and accept the self is the key to healing cancers."

(Quote ref. 87)   Francoise Sagan: *"Loving is not just caring deeply, it's, above all, understanding."*

(Quote ref. 88)   by John Patrick: *"Pain makes man think. Thought makes man wise. Wisdom makes life endurable."*

We had time to heal and think so that we could continue on all much the wiser. Yes, as I mentioned in my body section in chapter 13 - a cold sore I had was a very little thing, but it was a message, a message that needed to be paid more attention to. Everything starts out small and grows. How something or someone grows is determined by our attitudes, thought patterns and how we apply our lessons in everyday life. Stop, look and listen. Seek answers-move on.

I use to wonder how I would cope with my kids growing up and moving out. That alone would have been a mountain for me. Now, here I was separated, in a fairly new job, selling the house and practically everything in it, moving to a studio apartment and I was an empty nester. Talk about the unexpected! Didn't see all that coming, not in a billion years. This was all in less than 2 years, bombarded with stress, healing issues and empty nester syndrome. Ouch! Ouch! Ouch!

Anger is one letter short of danger. The Chinese character for crisis is danger and opportunity. This certainly holds true for us. If you don't pay attention to the red flags, gut feelings or what ever you want to call them, you can always count on the universe to step in and make you pay attention. Take time to be and stop, look and listen. Here's a quote of mine:

(Quote ref. 89) Nancy Lynn Martin-Author: *"All situations are meant to be learning experiences. You can go beyond what you think you can't be or do and you will be much stronger because of it."*

Crisis can become an opportunity, but you have to be aware of it and work through it. Going around will not gain a solution. You also have to go beyond getting around tuit and go through it.

(Quote ref. 90) Sufi Proverb: *"When the heart cries because of what it has lost, the spirit laughs for what it has found."*

(Bible quote ref. 17) Psalm 30:11-12 "You have turned my mourning into dancing; you have taken off my sackcloth and clothed me with joy, so that my soul may praise you and not be silent."

I have what I call the "gut law." When I don't feel right about something I go to (G) God. I then realize that I need to expect the (U) Unexpected. Next I go to my (T) Thoughts and go within (These are your constant companions). For my next step I go to (L) Laughter and see if my reasoning is on or off target. You will either laugh at yourself or laugh so that you don't cry. (When you become *aware* you will know what this means). I then go to (A) Awareness and hang out there for awhile and count my many blessings and realize that maybe this red flag is trying to tell me once again to stop, look and listen. Finally, I go to (W) Wisdom and connect all my experiences to what is going on and find out why I am feeling this way or why I have an ailment. Once again I have proven to myself that mind, body and soul are always connected.

This experience had a large impact on all of us. There is a reason for everything.

(Quote ref. 91) from Elisabeth Kubler-Ross: *"Learn to get in touch with the silence within yourself and know that everything in life has a purpose."*

We didn't realize at the time what was exactly happening, but as we continued to go through the stages of healing, we gradually saw the light at the end of the tunnel. We all still have a lot of work to do, but we are being more aware of everything. We're productive and on the road to recovery.

(Daily Word ref. 15) "Looking back on important events in my life, I understand that the intricate pieces have been joined together through a divine plan and purpose beyond any I would have been able to lay out for myself."

Don't get into the "why me?" mode. Why not you? You are a being that is here to grow. In order to grow you need to go through lessons. You are to rest and re-new yourself (BE) figure out what you need to change and go through it (not around it) and then get out there and (DO). Rest, think, do. This is the way that you build character qualities that make you an individual. You will be all the wiser for going through something. You will either give or receive (or both) a blessing for going through and being aware of the lesson.

(Quote ref. 92) by Bernice Johnson Reagon: *Life's challenges are not supposed to paralyze you, they're supposed to help you discover who you are.*

(Quote ref. 93) Gindu quote: *Do not ask God to make your life easier, ask him to show you how to be stronger.*

BEING: *"My Journal Time"* – What bullshit do you need to cleanup? Did you have any red flags or gut feelings today? If yes – what are you going to do about them? Do you have any open wounds that need healing? How are you going to handle them? Did you stop, look and listen today? What did you see and hear while you stopped and became a being (first) and a doer (second)?

My Journal

_____
_____
_____
_____
_____
_____
_____
_____
_____
_____
_____
_____
_____
_____
_____
_____
_____
_____
_____
_____
_____
_____
_____
_____
_____
_____
_____
_____
_____
_____
_____
_____
_____

My Journal

My Journal

Chapter 15

Boundaries

Boundaries take a lot of discipline. You have to train your mind to stay true to what you have set out to accomplish. This isn't as easy as you may think. You will encounter the dreaded snake again and the wolf in sheep's clothing. You will be tested on your boundaries mainly to learn that you really do care about yourself. Once you set your boundaries, be sure you stick to them, especially when you are dealing with other people.

We need to find the middle road of selfish and selfless. Maybe try (me-you) but keep up your self defense. Keep everything in balance and moderation. Everyone needs alone time to reach deep into their soul. Don't ever stretch yourself out so thin that you lose yourself. We need to go (within) once a day in order to re-connect. If you're not connected to yourself, how do you expect to be connected with others? It's okay to be a little selfish. Learn to love yourself and nourish your mind, body and soul.

I had a hard time with this for many years. Being a good mom was extremely important to me. Me time meant mom time to me because I enjoyed it so much. I was connected to myself but motherhood and family were my life, what I lived for. During my separation, I had a conversation with my sister-in-law Eileen. She said "Nancy, what did you do for yourself today?" I said "nothing." We talked awhile longer on the subject and I said I would do something special for myself that day. She called me up a couple hours later and said "Nancy, what are you doing for yourself? I said "nothing." I guess she caught me by surprise. I didn't do anything for myself but I didn't have an answer for why. Because she was thoughtful enough to call again to be sure I would start pampering myself, like now, not the next day, I started doing some enjoyable things for me, myself and I. Thanks Eileen, God bless you!

No matter if you throw yourself into family life, you're a workaholic, you're a community giver, a caregiver, or whatever, you need to set boundaries. Take time for you. There has to be down time in everything you do or you will get totally burnt out. Pampering yourself doesn't make you a bad person, it makes you refreshed and more at ease in what you're doing. It keeps you from getting burnt out and makes everything more manageable. It takes you off the merry – go – round so you can stop, look and listen. Rest – relax - renew.

(Book ref. 9) "*Why your Life Sucks*", Alan writes "If you do not set healthy boundaries, you cannot blame others for intruding on you. You are not a victim. You just didn't say No when you should have. Draw your lines well and your life will be your own."

(Quote ref. 94) by Pearl S. Buck: "*I love people. I love my family, my children but inside myself is a place where I live all alone and that's where you renew your springs that never dry up.*"

BOUNDARIES: "*My Journal Time*" – How did you find the middle road today? How were you selfish (in a good way?) How were you selfless (what did you do for someone else?) How did you reconnect with yourself today? Did you say YES when you wanted to say NO? Why?

My Journal

My Journal

My Journal

Chapter 16

Communication

Remember when I told you that I couldn't say my R's when I was young? Well, I also couldn't say a word that started with a soft J. I would say a hard G. You may think this wouldn't be a very big problem, but it was. It became very humiliating as a young girl. There happened to be a lot of soft (J's) in my life. My best friends were Jill and Joy, but I called them Gill and Goy. My cousins were Jimmy and Johnny – Gimmy and Gonny. A friend Julie-Gulie. Lord Jesus – Lord Gesus. My Godmothers were Jean and Joan – Gean and Goan. My favorite Disney character was Jiminy Cricket – Giminy Cricket. Jump rope was Gump rope. Jack in the box was Gack in the box. Jack and Jill was Gack and Gill. Jelly was Gelly. January, June and July – Ganuary, Goon and Guly. Juice was Goose. Jacket – was Gacket. So, from 5-9 years old I was the butt of all jokes – gokes.

To me, the most productive means of communication isn't what comes out of our mouths but what we wear on our mouths, a smile. Most of us also communicate with our eyes more so than with words. Mostly, however, I believe that an experience in itself is the very best means of communication. Words, more often than not seem to be a major source of most (if not all) of our misunderstandings. Even when listening to music, we sometimes misinterpret the lyrics. The song on top of my head that was misinterpreted was:

(Lyric ref. 24) *"Bad Moon Rising"* - "There's a bad moon on the rise" became "There's a bathroom on the right."

We can talk to our kids, or even some adults, until the cows come home. Do they understand what we are saying? When my kids were old enough to pick up after themselves, I talked to them about doing their share of keeping the house clean. I was a stay at home mom when they were little, so I had time to do everything but wanted to instill some form of responsibility in them and teach them self esteem. When they didn't keep up their rooms, I would say - "Who do you think I am – the maid?" I just assumed they knew what I was talking about. They kept their rooms cleaned up but a few months later my daughter Jenny came up to me and finally said "Mom, whats a maid?"

One day when my kids were young I was talking on the phone to a friend. She wanted to know if I had bought Easter candy and little gifts for the Easter baskets yet. I told her that I had so much Easter candy that I've got it coming out of my ears. When I woke up in the morning I had 6 eyes looking at my ears. I asked them what they were looking for in my ears. My oldest son Danny said "Easter candy." I said - "Easter candy?" He said - "Yeah you told someone on the phone that you had Easter candy coming out of your ears." Of course I explained to them that it was just a saying. I continued on to say that it was the same as when Jake, my youngest son, pictured a nose with legs when I explained that when you have a cold – your nose runs.

(Book ref. 20) *"Free to be you and me"* by Marlo Thomas was taken down once again from the book shelf to help explain. Thank you Marlo! Some years later Jake was in a "Free to be you and me" musical at school.

Just recently, Jenny told me that when she was little she wondered why her dad and I disobeyed street signs. She went on to say that the road sign said *Do not pass* but that we would just keep passing the sign anyway. Another time we were in between homes. A house deal fell through and we had already given notice at our apartment. We were staying by my husbands mothers house. After calling about numerous apartments inquiring if they took 3 kids and a dog, I found one that said yes. I called everyone together and said, "Come on and get in the car, I found someone that takes kids and dogs." We all were in the car and I looked in the back seat and saw 3 kids with tears in their eyes. When I asked them what was wrong, they said "Why are you taking us by people who are going to take us?"

You can listen to people, you can try to understand their feelings, and by all means don't stop being there for others, but to actually experience and ask what they are trying to communicate - this is the only way that you can even come close to knowing what someone is thinking. Children teach you to say what you mean and explain everything. Never assume someone is taking something the way you think they are.

Having group sessions with people that share a common thread recover from something faster than those who try doing it solo. Sharing stories give you ideas on how to handle things. Be the teacher and the student. Get things out in the open and be open minded to everything in life. Always expect the unexpected and don't assume anything. Share stories for inspiration and encouragement.

(Lyrics ref. 25) *"Take me there"* - "And I wanna go down every road you been – Where your hopes and dreams and wishes live. What made you who you are – Tell me what your story is."

Always do your best to understand the other person. If you are confused about something, ask them to be more specific in what they are trying to express. Be as clear as you can be when you are talking to others. Communication has three parts: listening, talking and a whole lot of love. Teens, please open up to parents or someone you trust. You are not alone on anything. Keep communication lines open.

When my kids were small and acted up or I don't think what they are doing now is within their best interest, I tell them - "I love you, but I don't like what you are doing." I've always been big on saying consequences of your actions. It seems to have made them stop, look and listen. I use to have family meetings to sort out everyones feelings. You can guide them by suggesting what to do, put it out there for them to think about, but they are going to want to try things out themselves. What they do or don't do will never change my love for them. I will not love one more than the other because of what they do or don't do. I believe that this eliminates a lot of jealousy and competition among them. Attention getting is eliminated because there isn't any comparing involved. What happens to them is based on their individual decisions and choices. What ever they decide - I will always love them unconditionally.

A couple of years ago I told Jenny if she doesn't anchor her Christmas tree to the wall before putting her ornaments on, it might fall. She had just bought several Disney ornaments that she added to her collection.

When I got to her apartment there was a note that said "Tree fell just like you said it would. When will I learn to listen to my mommy. It broke 4 good ornaments. Watch when you walk in the living room, there may be glass from the bells from Disney." (Consequences of your actions). Always keep communicating, it will sink in when the student is ready. This of course goes for everybody- child-teen-adult.

When all of us were working starting in the mid 1990's, we communicated by notes. We all worked different shifts and didn't see too much of one another. Here are a few priceless ones. When I was working at a community college – Jake left this on my windshield at work: Dated 9-8-98 "Hey mom – just driving by and thought I'd tell you Hi and I love you, see you around 9:30-10:00 - Always Jake." Dated 10- 2000 "Going to Jared's for weekend, call my cell phone tonight if you need me - Jake." Dated 9-97 "Mom, thanks for listening – Love Jake - your son." Dated 3-5-99 "Went to pick up art supplies-Happy Birthday Dad- Later – Jake." Dated 2-13-00 "Mommy - Look in the fritter fratter (refrigerator) to see what I found. Happy Valentines Day – Love Jenny." Dated 2-13-00 "Dad – Thank you for taping Felicity and Jack and Jill- even though I forgot to ask you to – Love Jenny." Dated 4-21-98 "Rusty (our dog) ate and got a biscuit-Love Jenny."

As far as communication on global terms, I have this to say. We are in dire need of being more tactful/more agreeable. Everyone needs to work at coming to agreements.

Wake up people before it's too late. Global problems begin with non communication and fear. The key word that everyone is ignoring is diplomacy. Has everyone become so callous that they can't even come to agreements? Negotiations bring win – win. Violence and war are unproductive and bring win – lose or lose - combative situations and onto retaliation which can go on forever.

(Quote ref. 95) Nancy Lynn Martin – Author: *"The trouble with the world is that some of us forget to put the index finger up along side the middle finger. Do it, and than turn your hand around. Peace to all."*

Ants are more advanced then we are for Gods sake. We could learn a lot from an ant- they all work together, remember? Think about it.

They are the size of 1/3 of one of our pinky finger nails, yet more advanced then we are. How does that make you feeeeel??

COMMUNICATION: *"My Journal Time"* – What did you do today that strengthened your communication skills? How are you trying to understand people better? Did you assume the meaning of something someone said? If YES – why didn't you ask them to clear up the misunderstanding? What is your solution to GLOBAL communication?

My Journal

My Journal

My Journal

Chapter 17

Compare /Competition

We are all unique in our own way. Why would anyone even think of being in a competition. Any type of competition is just a way of sucking the life force right out of you. Competing is missing the whole point of DNA. We are all individuals, no two of us the same, just like snowflakes, no two the same. Each one of us is an original. There is no comparison. Say that you are happy dancing. All of a sudden you see someone doing moves you like and you do them and you like how you feel. Thats fine – do it. If it feels good – do it. If, however, you choose to compete with someone dancing and they win the competition, does that mean you should stop dancing the way you dance and dance the way the winner did in order to win something? I'm sorry, but you're not winning anything, you are losing yourself and who you are.

Same goes for sports. Why can't people just play for the fun of it? Why does it have to be a competition where one score out does the other. My teams better then your team is totally uncalled for. I don't see anyone learning (team work) from any of the games. Sometimes it gets so out of control that people get hurt. Battles even get into something that is supposed to be fun and good exercise. Stop the violence.

May I rest my case when people are being hurt or even murdered in these so called competitions. Enough is enough, its just another form of war. Play for fun and have raffles for community gains only. The money spent on competitive sports, not even counting the betting that goes on, is totally outrages. Appreciate how different we all are and love the differences. Stop the nah nah nah nah – I'm better then you crap. We all contribute to the world in our own way. The trophy, recognition or money you receive in a competition say nothing of who you are as a human being, nothing at all.

(Lyrics ref. 26)   From the movie *Cars*: *"Find Yourself"* - "Well you go through life so sure of where you're heading and you wind up lost – and its the best thing that could happen – cause sometimes when you lose your way – it's really just as well – cause you find yourself – that's when you find yourself."

If you haven't seen the Disney movie – see it! It is filled with morals of how to be a caring compassionate friend. No trophy can take the place of friendships, love and being your self.

(Book ref. 21)   *"12 Secrets of Highly Creative Women"* by Gail Mcmeekin "For so many of us, breaking free of our societal and psychological chains is a prerequisite to truly creating a life that expresses our genuineness and uniqueness."

A skater does a good routine an hour before going out for the gold. She falls down during her main performance and the gold goes to someone else. Then the judges add insult to injury and say – oh poor so in so – she did a good routine during practice but couldn't quite pull it off when it counts. Just stop it people, enough is enough!!   I watch Dancing with the Stars on TV. I enjoy the dancing, but when the judges start talking and they do the scoring, I close my ears and sing Lalalala. I'm not interested in the judging part. I watch other competitions also but never the judging part. Most of it is demoralizing, not encouraging. Don't even get me started on what I think of child modeling competitions.

COMPETITION: *"My Journal Time"* - What are your views on competition? Do you compete? If YES – how do you feel when you are competing and what do you expect from the competition? How does it make you feel when you (LOSE?) (WIN?) Why do you compete? If you could just do what ever you're doing for the fun of it – would you enjoy it more?

My Journal

My Journal

My Journal

Chapter 18

Different Drummers
Nonconformists
Creativity

If you have accomplished being a different drummer and can smile when someone laughs at you, then you have discovered true happiness and joy.

(Quote ref. 96) by Unknown: *"Intoxicate yourself with an ecstatic experience. Be weird."*

(Quote ref. 97) by Henry David Thoreau: *"If a man does not keep pace with his companions, perhaps it is because he hears a different drummer. Let him step to the music he hears, however measured or far away."*

Remember when I said you have to go back to your childhood often and re-learn and to remember? Well, remember what made you happy as a child. Becoming an adult does not mean stop being happy, yet many think that if they do something childish that they will be called childish or to grow up. We lose who we are. Grown-ups are afraid to be silly. Some think that they have to drink in order to let loose, then they feel they have an excuse to be silly.

Have you ever watched kids play house – play grown-ups? Watch them next time. They change their little faces to an overworked look. They get all serious and the boy will put on a tie and the girl will wear high heels. They sigh a lot and they get grumpy. Why do men wear ties, why do they walk around with a noose around their neck all day? And why do women walk around in pain with tight high heels and tight clothes, not to mention those teddies. What about underwear up their butts? These are full time wedgees and highly unsanitary.

And guys, we don't need to see your underwear when you walk around with your pants hanging on your thighs. None of these things are comfortable.

If kids don't pick this behavior up at home then they pick it up on the TV or in movies. Think about movies you see and adults don't look very happy do they? Even if it's a comedy there is usually some type of dilemma being solved, but in a comical way. And then the soap opras, there isn't any happiness in those dang shows. Then they see the news or rag magazines, no happiness there either. The media only talks about the disasters of the day, how often do you hear about the good things in your community or in the world?

Be your own drummer and don't get stuck in what I call society norms. Who wants to be normal? Not me, the more different I am, the happier I am. When I was in school I never concerned myself with what peers thought. So what- Who kaz (cares) was my motto. Peer pressure is a form of stress and needs to be avoided in any way, shape and form.

(Lyrics ref. 27) *"Free to be you and me"* - "Every boy on this land grows to be his own man. In this land, every girl grows to be her own woman. Take my hand, come with me where the children are free. Come with me, take my hand, and we'll run."

Tell others to stop and find themselves and to leave you alone. Do not entertain any form of such negativity and what others think of you. Stay true to yourself. I use to think and still do think that it is sad that some people can't think of better things to do than to show you how insecure they actually are, that they have to pick on you!! Not only that- but it's unloving and unkind, so if you are reading this and you pick people apart- "stop it." Everyone needs to continue listening to the rhythm and beat of their own drum. This is what brings joy to you and keeps your mind, body and soul alive. It's what keeps you an individual and what gives you a unique character and helps you be a creative person.

(Lyrics ref. 28) *"Flashdance"* – *"What a Feeling"* - "Well, I hear the music, close my eyes, feel the rhythm, wrap around, take a hold of my heart. Take your passion and make it happen."

Since I'm on the subject of dancing I'd like to say a few words about the movie Dirty Dancing. Not only is the music and dancing fantastic – but the plot is so true to real life and how people are so quick at slapping on labels – when they know nothing about a person or a situation. If you assume – then get on the awareness path.

(Bible ref. 14) Matthew 7:1-2 "Judge not, that you be not judged. For with what judgment you judge, you will be judged; and with the measure you use, it will be measured back to you."

I use to play school, library, and dolls the most. I also played store with my parents record albums. I would set up my grandmothers Daily Word booklets on the bed and line them up like rows of desks. I usually played library and dolls outside in a tent made by putting a big blanket over the wash line and holding it down with bricks. I love being outside, it makes me feel more like the free spirit that I am. Sleeping outside is like freedom to me. I had a very vivid imagination and actually believed I was a teacher, librarian and mother.

I use to love watching my grandmother. Just knowing that she was a dancer at the Pabst Theater in Milwaukee, Wisconsin and seeing her back bend photos and pretty yet comfortable costumes, gave me goosebumps. She also played the piano with such determination that her fingers would just seem to sashay across the keys and I couldn't help but to get up and dance. Rustles of Spring, Clair de Lune, Liebestraum and Sound of Music were her favorites. It didn't matter how I danced, I just danced. To this day I feel total freedom when I dance and I don't care what I look like - Who kaz!

(Quote ref. 98) Famous quote: several versions. *"Dance as though no one is watching you, Love as though you have never been hurt before, Sing as though no one can hear you, Live as though heaven is on earth."*

I know I instilled dancing and music in my home for my kids. I totally loved to watch them dance, it was the true happiness of motherhood for me, my utmost favorite thing to do. Everything they played involved some type of dance or form of creative imagination. I lived to see what they were going to create next. Little beings having fun doing silly and creative things. The sillier, the better. My daughter and I dance together when we get together now, laugh and do silly things. One day she said, "Remember when you use to say: Home again- home again jiggitty jig jig jig?" The other day my son called and said that his girlfriend was pushing the shopping cart behind him and he was stopping, so he put his arms out behind him and wiggled his fingers. He said he remembered me doing that and now he was doing it (just out of the blue). The last time I visited my son out in California we got him on video dancing in his kitchen. Brings back great memories and the hope of more to come.

(Quote ref. 99) by Santayana: *"A person who has never done something silly will never do anything interesting."*

Cherished idiosyncrasies are the cornerstones of family and individuality, society can't give you that when they want everyone to act the same. We're all supposed to look like a model, dress a certain way, act a certain way, get a face lift after 50, basically be robots - I guess. I grew up in the 50's when high heels were a big thing. All women wore them. Even bedroom slippers were heels, how insane is that? I remember my mom saying her feet hurt as she would take her heels off. I would say "Then don't wear them." My dad would come home from work and quickly take his tie and suit off and put on comfortable clothes. I couldn't for the life of me understand why people would do things that brought on a sad face. Be a different drummer – wear tennies and soft white cotton socks, not those itchy nylon ones - be comfy – be kind to your feet. Wear comfy free flowing clothes that are made of non itchy fabric. Maybe tight clothes and teddies are sexy, but they certainly aren't comfortable. See through light cotton t-shirts are just as sexy, and ooh so comfy.

Albert Einstein is known for his curiosity and his idiosyncrasies. He was slow at school and told he would never amount to much. He was happy when he saw unity in his thoughts. He said to a friend that he will never grow old , he had a vivid imagination. He was truly a different drummer who used his talent from above to the utmost positivity for himself and others.

There was a guy at my husbands place of work that ignored the remarks about him not having a car. For many years he rode his bike to work and was very frugal in all ways. Everyone at work complained about cars breaking down and bills. He was the different drummer that one day gave them something to think about. He said he just bought a house. Everyone was shocked that he would pay out interest on a house-that was so unlike him. He went on to say he payed cash for the house. He didn't care what people thought of him, he had a plan and he stuck to it, different drummer, yes, happy?? Extremely!!

(Quote ref. 100) by Sam Keen: *"The still, small voice of God never calls on me to be like another man. It appeals to me to rise to my full stature and fulfill the promise that sleeps within my being."*

I was talking to a woman one day who just had her nails done. She said she felt sick the whole time from the smell. When I asked her why she does it – she said because it seems to make her lady friends happy when they have theirs done. I told her she needs to walk to the beat of a different drummer and find out what makes her feel good. She said she likes dancing to silly music, you know- the bunny hop – the funky chicken – Y.M.C.A. We were in a mall when she said that. Can you guess what I did? I started doing the funky chicken right then and there, and she couldn't help but to join in and so did a bunch of other people. We continued on with the other 2 dances as well. Differerent drummers unite, true happiness rules. Remember love, laugh, learn.

(Lyrics ref. 29) *"Dance to the Music"* – "All we need is a drummer, for people who only need a beat. I'm gonna add a little guitar and make it easy too move your feet."

One day, back in the 60's, my mom, sister and I were reading about chinese animal astrology. We found out that I am a rabbit, my mom is a horse, and my sister an ox. We continued to read about the animals and our characteristic traits. All of a sudden we thought it would be silly to act out our animal signs. I started hopping around from chair to chair asking for carrots and twitching my nose. My mom went by the kitchen sink and drank water out of it like a horse by a trough and pranced around making neigh sounds. My sister got on top of the buffet and tied a long winter scarf to the phone and to her waist as if she was pulling it around and she was making snorting sounds. Just then, grandma walked in from walking the dog. When we explained what we were doing, she found out she was an ox. She joined in, put the dog leash around her waist and had the dog in tow, as if she was an ox. We had music on (as always) and our birds were chirpin like crazy. If any body else would have seen this scene, I'm sure they would have called the men in the white coats. But we had a good time frolicking around, laughing like crazy and totally letting loose - so - who kaz (cares). Who needs drugs or alcohol when you have imaginations like this? And besides, when you do something without drugs or alcohol, you remember it!!

(Quote ref. 101) Unknown: *"Blessed is the man who can laugh at himself, for he will never cease to be amused."*

(Lyrics ref. 30) *"Return to Innocence"* - " Don't care what people say. Just follow your own way. Don't give up and use the chance. To return to innocence."

DIFFERENT DRUMMERS: *"My Journal Time"* – List all the things you enjoyed as a child. Are you doing any of them now? If NOT – WHY NOT? Students – do you let your peers make you change your mind and go against your true self? If YES – Why? (It's your life not theirs). Remember – you're responsible for your reactions to everything. You don't need peers that want you to go against your true self – nobody needs friends like that – no matter what your age. What idiosyncrasies do you have? What silly thing/s did you do today? How did you feel? Didn't do anything silly? WHY NOT?

My Journal

My Journal

My Journal

Chapter 19

Diversity

During a 25th high school reunion, these were seven different answers to the question: What have you been doing since high school? Well, first I met up with Amy and we walked down to the old drugstore on Maple Street and got an old fashioned soda. Next, we got in her car and drove downtown to the Oasis and took in a movie. Then we got a bite to eat and then drove up and down the strip. She then drove me home and I went to bed. The next day was a Saturday and I slept in till noon and then showered. Next, I walked my dog and then took a bike ride to the lake. Some of the old gang was down there playing volleyball, so I joined in and then went home. Next day I went to church, ate ham and rolls and then got things ready for my first day of work. This conversation did not stop here. She goes on to recap everything she has done for the last 25 years.

Ah, not much, got a job at the dairy plant, still work there. I'm married, have a nice wife and 2 kids. Thats about it. I'm 43 now, not much more to do.

Went to college. Have a nice home over on Monroe Avenue. This is my wife Karen. We have 3 kids. I'm working my way up the ladder at a progressing company. We like to entertain and travel. We camp and go to the lake where we have a houseboat.

Oh man – are you sure you want to hear this? Things went down fast after school, I thought school days were a bummer, but life, it just sucks. Now when I think back on school days, they were the best years of my life. Things are so hard in (the real world) car is breaking down all the time, kids get into trouble. Bills, bills, bills.

I'm single – never married – I do clerical work and I like to travel. I am dating someone kind of special now.

I take one day at a time. I'm president of a growing company that sells office machines – I have a wonderful family that I adore – I would like to get a home based business going so I can have more time with my family and retire from my job. I would love to have more time and freedom to use my talents – all in all – my life is good.

You know me – a go-getter from day 1. I became a doctor and own a winter home and a summer home. I'm divorced with 2 kids who are married. I have 6 classic cars, tons of stuff – but I'm not happy. Sometimes I wish I could just have a simpler life that I could enjoy instead of doctoring all the time – you know – have time with the kids and grandkids – maybe find a special person to share life with.

Some people see someone their age with a new car, nice family and successful job and they will say "Why does that guy deserve all that and I don't have it – what did he do?" "Why does he seem so positive about life and I think life sucks?" We don't know what other people are thinking or what kind of life they have unless we ask. We assume things of others when we don't know their situation. If you do ask questions, however, and the other party would rather not answer them, that is their right. This all falls under-the grass is not always greener over there. It also falls under it's all in your way of thinking, learning your lessons, and choices. There are no two people that have exactly the same life. Sure there are things we do that are the same as others, but not even twins have exactly the same day to day life – there are always differences. Everything in your life is for a reason and accomplished when the time is right for you. Enjoy your journey and don't worry about the life of another. You don't know what others have been through. If you want to know others cultures then ask and go on from there to learn more.

Never be jealous of anything or anybody. Everybody has their own life and you need to say live and let live. Bless everyone and enjoy the camaraderie with people of all lands and notice that a smile and laughter are universal.

(Lyrics ref. 31) *"Take the Time"* fits this situation: "Each of us has come here with a story of our own...We come from different places and the pain has different names. With different circumstances but the feelings are the same, take the time to love somebody."

(Lyrics ref. 32) *"What's going on"* - "Ah you know we've got to find a way to bring some understanding here today-to bring some lovin here today."

(Lyrics ref. 33) *"Teardrop"* - "(Love) love is a verb-love is a doing word."

(Daily Word ref. 16) "Each has the divine potential to grow into countless combinations of abilities, given and developed. The world is blessed by the diversity of its people."

It all comes down to love - people. Love- laugh -learn – see how everything connects?

(Daily Word ref. 17) "Today let us celebrate our uniqueness as well as our unity with one another."

(Bible ref. 19)   1 Corinthians 12: 4-6   "There are diversities of gifts, but the same spirit. There are differences of ministries, but the same Lord. And there are diversities of activities, but it is the same God who works all in all."

DIVERSITY: *"My Journal Time"* – If you are under 43 – what do you think your answer would be to the question – What did you do after graduation? If you are over 43 what is your answer? List some of your stories that make you the unique individual that you are. What ways can you think of to bring more understanding and love into the world today? What are some of the ways you can bring a POSITIVE MODE into your life and into your diversified environment?

My Journal

My Journal

My Journal

Chapter 20

Dreams

I'm not going to tell you about following your dreams, because we already know that we should find out what our assignment in life is and by following that, we will be doing the work we love and will be spreading love and serving others. You may not get the dream the way you thought you would, so be aware of everything. The universe has the final say. You will have your dream but look for other ways other than your way. You may be surprised with the outcome.

What I want to tell you about here is nighttime dreams. I know this comes along with a lot of skepticism as does the issue of astrology and psychics. Remember what I said at the beginning of this journey book : keep only what will nourish you, and stay open minded. Try it first and if it does't work for you then delete it, weed it out.

I can understand why people have no belief in dreams having any meaning. The unconscious can be a very complex and tricky thing to deal with. It's right up there with the stars and your astrological chart being crazy, right? Dreams, I believe are messages and I keep a dream diary. The best book I have found to interpret your dreams is:

(Book ref. 22) *"The Element Encyclopedia of 20,000 Dreams"* by Theresa Cheung

If you really want to get into your dreams read:

(Book ref. 23) *"Book of Dreams"* by Sylvia Browne. Included in her book are the 5 different kinds of dreams, dreams of people and interpretations of some dreams. She also mentions that there are 121 references to dreams in the Bible.

(Lyrics ref. 34) It has been written that Paul Mccartney wrote the song *"Yesterday"* after having a dream and waking up with a tune in his head.

He didn't have the lyrics – and at first they were "Scrambled eggs, oh my baby, how I love your legs."

You won't remember your dreams, so you have to have paper and pen by your bed. Jot down key words of what you remember when you wake up, even if it's 2 a.m. Don't think you'll remember them in the morning, because you won't. In the morning look up the words in a dream book. I transfer mine to a notebook so that I have about a years worth in one book. Pay special attention to repeats. Those might have the strongest messages that you should pay attention to in your waking life. Sigmund Freud believed dreams were the road to the unconscious. Carl Jung believed dreams were a path to spirituality. God's revelations to the prophets were usually by visions.

(Bible ref. 20) Numbers 12:6 "I the Lord make myself known to them in visions; I speak to them in dreams."

Also, back to astrology. The three wise men were astrologers.

(Bible ref. 21) Matthew 2:9 "When they heard the king, they departed; and behold, the star which they had seen in the East went before them, till it came and stood over where the young Child was."

Astrology is " the study of the supposed influence of the stars and planets on human affairs." Astronomy is "the general science of all celestial bodies."

(Quote ref. 102) by Rabindranath Tagore: *I slept and dreamt that life was a joy, I awoke and saw that life was service, I acted and behold, service was joy.*

I had what I call a spirituality dream in 2002. My bedroom at the time had a huge window behind the headboard. (If you are into feng shui- you know this is not good placement.) Non conformist Nancy strikes again. I liked it because with the huge window open I felt like I was sleeping outside. I did put the red ribbon across the window, like feng shui suggests. Anyway, back to the dream. There were birds, rabbits, squirrels, deer, a wolf, moose, fox, elk, goats, a donkey, a horse, a bear, sheep, antelope, etc. The dream was like totally real. The animals were outside my window frolicking back and forth the length of the house with complete freedom. When I woke up and looked outside my window, it was almost as if I could see the aftermath of my dream and then they slowly disappeared. I believe that this was the start of my awakening to my spiritual journey of life.

When I looked up each animal in the dream dictionary, each one mentioned something about getting in touch with self. This was during the time of my separation from my husband. The dream was telling me: this is the time to go within and that is exactly what I did. Once again: divine order. There is a time for everything and a reason for everything. A time to sow and a time to reap. I was entering the process of total renewal. The (Goat) symbol was very awakening for me. The interpretation was: Adversity overcome through powers of patience. I will climb and survive difficulties. The (Horse): Limitless nature of self. The (Bear) was: Be alone to think. And the (Deer): Great friendship with messengers from the unconscious.

(Daily Word ref. 18) "I am growing spiritually through life as You lead me to my mountaintop experiences of awareness."

So, give it a try, interpret your dreams. See if they connect to what is happening in your life. Sometimes dreams give you that special little push you need to change something that you are in denial about in waking hours. As far as astrology goes, in the 70's, the line was "So what's your sign?" Now you're supposed to know your jupiter sign too. Your Jupiter sign is what gives you your descriptive potential ways to grow. Where all the other planets were when you were born also have something to do with who you are. My Jupiter is in Aries which means I am inspired and inspiring and self promoting. I also need to slow down and be more Zen like. My sun sign is Sagittarius, but recently I found out that not only am I Sagittarius, but I am also Ophiuchus. Only people born between November 29 and December 17 fit into this 13th zodiac sign.

Leave it to me to be born during these few days of oh-fee-yoo-cuss. Maybe that is why I am such a way out drummer and free spirit. Some of the characteristics of an Ophiuchus are that they like to heal self and others. They are good talkers and listeners. Cast light where there is dark, but need to take time to relax and be aware of snakes in the grass. I call myself "sag-ari-yoocus".

At any rate, astrology and dreams seem to have a connection into our minds and how we think and act. Dreams interpret your most inner thoughts. They are messengers getting your attention while you sleep because you may be too busy to get other messages during waking hours. You won't appreciate your world of dreams unless you remove the doubt you have about them. Lets say you look up the meaning of a dream and it means something negative. You say this is crazy and that your not going to do it anymore. This is when you have to ask yourself why you don't want to look into the negative meaning. What nerve did it hit that you are in denial about? This is when you need to go within and see the opportunity of the (so called negative) meaning.

When you look into your astrological birth chart, some books and internet sites give you ideas to challenge certain aspects of your sign in order to improve the direction of your life. Again, always look into your Jupiter sign along with your Sun sign. And of course if you are totally not into this, then delete it.

DREAMS: *"My Journal Time"* – Start a dream notebook. You don't have to buy an interpretation book if you just want to try it first. You can look up the words on the internet on a dream site. Before you go to bed ask for a problem to be looked into. Record your dream and see if there is a connection. Do this for several months. If you don't think it will do anything for you – then weed it out. Check out your jupiter sign and combine it with your zodiac sun sign. It just might give you that extra boost to gain new ways of growth. Sun sign = personality. Jupiter sign = motivation.

My Journal

My Journal

My Journal

Chapter 21

Emotional Baggage

This is going to be short and sweet. The best way I can describe it, is to compare it with the ebb and tide of the ocean. I call emotional baggage (EBB) Energy Bureaucracy Burnout. It declines, robs and controls your positive energy life forces. We are to live positively with the high tide where the water is moving and flowing. Some people spend too much on EBB instead of opening up more productive energy by ditching the negative emotional baggage. We all have baggage, the key word is forgive. Forgive yourself and forgive others. If you have emotional baggage, get it out of your life. Get rid of guilt, regrets, negativity and wallowing. Just get your butt in gear and get on with your life. Learn the lessons and apply them to your life. And by all means don't talk about past negative experiences with new people that you meet. Don't be a pity seeker. If you're not over someone or something, then take more time to regroup before starting a new relationship.

EMOTIONAL BAGGAGE: *"My Journal Time"* - Get your butt in gear and regroup. Spend time by your self. List things that you can do to become more aware of situations that are not for your best interest. Make a contract with yourself stating how you are making changes based on what you have learned.

My Journal

_____

_____
_____
_____
_____
_____
_____
_____
_____
_____
_____
_____
_____
_____
_____
_____
_____
_____
_____
_____
_____
_____
_____
_____
_____
_____
_____

My Journal

My Journal

Chapter 22

Forgiveness

Read emotional baggage again. Also I would like to add, if you still can't forgive someone or something, ask yourself where you are still hurting. When we don't forgive, we are actually hurting ourselves more. When you keep past hurts, anger, guilt or whatever bottled up, you are playing havoc with your mind, body and soul. One good way of giving your hurts the boot out is to write them on stones. Say you need to forgive someone for something they said to you. Write their name on the stone and chant a few words about the situation. When you're done with all the stones (that's if you have several things or people to forgive, including yourself) take the stones to a high hill or lake. Be sure no one will get hurt when you throw the stone off the hill or in the water. Say good bye, I forgive, as you throw it.

If you still can't forgive, than seek professional help. First, try to understand the situation. Second, show compassion for self and others. Third, forgive and then you will heal. Sometimes you will get a sort of pop-quiz. You may think you have forgiven someone when low and behold you are again triggered by something. You need to go back and see why someones behavior or an event is still making you crazy. You need to go back and do some more life work and do more inventory of the issue.

(Bible ref. 22) Matthew 5:44 - "But I say to you, love your enemies, bless those who curse you, do good to those who hate you, and pray for those who spitefully use you and persecute you."

(Daily Word ref. 19) "With a forgiving attitude, I experience more moments of inner peace, more moments of physical calm, more moments of pure joy. Forgiveness prepares me to give and receive the love of God that heals all hurt."

When you forgive, you free up energy for more productive living. But, if you don't want to forgive, then don't. It's your choice. If you want to stay stuck, then put up with the unproductive path that *you* put yourself on. It's up to you to change your life, it's all in your thoughts and the action that you take!! Cause and effect.

The power is within you: not a bottle of pills, a needle, alcohol, wallowing in depression or anything else you do against your mind, body and soul. Take the responsibility for yourself and make a positive change in you life instead of trying to go around with temporary solutions. Forgiving self and others heals. Everything else brings on more problems. Non forgiveness puts you back in that damn rocking chair again, it doesn't get you anywhere. You should only be in a rocking chair for soothing pampering purposes and rocking your babies. That's a rocking chairs purpose.

For example: When you look that bottle in the face next time or want a pity party, ask yourself "Am I doing this because I can't forgive, fill in the blank?" Face what the obstacle is and move forward or you will stay stuck. Release the hurt, bless it for the lesson it gave you and move on. Forgiveness rids negative energy.

(Quote ref. 103) Saint Francis of Assisi prayed: *"Lord, make me an instrument of Thy peace. Where there is injury let me sow pardon."*

(Daily Word ref. 20) "As I forgive, I clear away any debris from the past incidents, conversations, and actions. I create an atmosphere in which healing takes place as understanding, cooperation, and agreement."

(Daily Word ref. 21) "Now there is a place in my heart, in my mind, and in my life for new positive experiences. As I forgive, I open ways for me to enjoy new and fulfilling opportunities and adventures."

FORGIVENES: *"My Journal Time"* - Is there a lesson you need to relearn? Are you unable to forgive someone or something because you have wounds to heal? How are you going to get past the hurt and onto the heal?

My Journal

My Journal

My Journal

Chapter 23

Fear

Fear stands for (false expectations appearing real) or (false evidence appearing real). You either fear something that you expect is going to happen or you fear something that is based on something that is untrue. Think about the things that you fear and they will fit into one of these. Look the fear in the face, learn the lesson and look for the opening in the door for the next lesson and move on!

Knowing this, you should be able to figure out how to eliminate fear in your life. Fear is just an obstacle again to make you once again be aware and stop, look, listen. Look the fear in the face and stand up to it. You can do more than you think you can.

Remember when I feared being an "empty nester". Not only was I an empty nester but I was given other mountains to climb, and all at the same time! Kids grow and we all grow, it's not something to fear, it's something that needs to be. It's called life. I turned my obstacle, fear and adversity into a healing opportunity for positive change. My marriage relationship is extremely negative. My husband is a negative person and I am positive. We still need to keep our boundaries up so that we do not drain each other with our differences. My husband and I are on totally different paths, always were, always will be. The universe said, you don't think you can do something? Well, let me show you that you can do it, plus make changes in other areas of your life. Not only that, but you can do them all at the same time. As I took baby steps and progressed, my faith grew stronger.

Remember the story of Chicken Little – The Sky is Falling? She feared that the sky was falling after an acorn fell on her head. Fear got the best of her to the point that her body language triggered the sly fox to take advantage of her and her friends. The sly fox, Foxy Loxy, was the snake in the grass. Chicken little ran to tell the king that the sky was falling but came across Henny Penny, Ducky Lucky, Goosey Loosey, Turkey Lurkey. When they all come upon Foxy Loxy, he tells all of them to follow him and he leads them to the woods, straight to his den. They never got to the king. Don't let fear get the best of you. Don't run around like a (chicken with your head cut off). No one can think straight in chaos.

(Quote ref. 104) by Susan Jeffers: *"We cannot escape fear. We can only transform it into a companion that accompanies us on all our exciting adventures. Take a risk a day, one small or bold stroke that will make you feel great once you have done it."*

FEAR: *"My Journal Time"* - What do you fear? Is it a fear based on the unknown or something that you really don't know to be the truth? If you don't know something – what can you do to learn more? Can you go out there and risk a little to see if you can do what you think you can't do? List your fears and activate the fear into a positive force. Have faith that the universe is behind you 100%.

My Journal

_____
_____
_____
_____
_____
_____
_____
_____
_____
_____
_____
_____
_____
_____
_____
_____
_____
_____
_____
_____
_____
_____
_____
_____
_____
_____
_____
_____
_____
_____
_____

My Journal

My Journal

Chapter 24

Faith

After I took small steps, I realized that I could do what I thought I couldn't and the more I did, the more faith I gained. Did I have anxiety? Sure. Did I fear the unknown? You bet. But as I moved forward I said to myself "Nancy, you are not respecting your mind, body and soul by having anxiety and fear. Those things are unproductive. Let go and let God. I am in this to learn and grow and change an unproductive path, to a productive one." I gained the faith of a mustard seed.

(Bible ref. 23) Matthew 17:20 "If you have faith the size of a mustard seed, you will say to this mountain, 'Move from here to there,' and it will move; and nothing will be impossible for you."

Have faith that everything happens for a reason and that the universe has everything under control in its divine order.

(Daily Word ref. 22) "I trust that the best outcome will develop in the perfect way and at the optimum time."

(Daily Word ref. 23) "Through faith, I know that God's power is greater than any circumstance, and with faith, I can see new possibilities where none appeared to be."

When you go through lessons and learn from them, the universe sends you more lessons. You are never given anything that you can not handle. Have faith that you can and will climb every mountain that is given to you.

(Quote ref. 105) by Barbara Winter: *"When you come to the edge of all the light you know, and are about to step off into the darkness of the unknown, faith is knowing one of two things will happen. There will be something solid to stand on, or you will be taught how to fly."*

(Bible ref. 24)   Ephesians 10-17: The whole armor of god, shield of faith - (meaning of)   belt on waist -truth, breastplate – righteousness, feet – gospel of peace, shield – faith, helmet – salvation, sword - spirit word of god (the bible).

FAITH: *"My Journal Time"* – List the times that you had obstacles and you learned a lesson from them. Write your feelings on how you went through the lessons and then ultimately realized that you were stronger. List ways of how you can continue keeping that faith.

My Journal

My Journal

My Journal

Chapter 25

Family

A family is defined as: one's own spouse, parents, children, relatives and ancestors. But it is also defined as: a group of things with some common feature. It is any group of people that are together to provide harmony, understanding, respect, empathy, compassion and unconditional love. If you don't have family, for whatever reason, you can always find people out in the world. Just remember what you learned and apply it to relationships. Join clubs with people that have the same interests as you. Seek friendships in your church and at work. Any relationship that entails harmony, understanding, respect, empathy, compassion and unconditional love is family. People that nourish your mind, body and soul and do not drain you or bring negativity into your life are considered family. You need to put your boundaries in action if anyone is bringing negative forces into your life.

(Daily Word ref. 24) "As family members, we are blessed with an awareness of one anothers needs and desires. We share understanding and support."

When I worked at Disney, my favorite restaurant was Ohana. It is hawaiian and before they seat you, they explain that we are all family. They ask your name and then announce you as cousin (your name). They have a session for kids where they play games. It is a good feeling place that makes you feel like you are at a family reunion. Not only that, the food is out of this world, scrumptiously delicious.

The one thing that I want to stress here is the word perfect. Don't use the word perfect in any way, shape or form. Don't ever expect perfection from yourself or anyone else. We're here to do the best we can, but don't stretch that out to be perfect.

In Genesis we are told that God created the heavens and the earth. Each day that He created something He finished with "that it was good." He never said perfect, but He said good or very good. We are all here to learn and be of service, do the best we can and at the end of each day, bless everything. Be thankful for everything and say "and it was all good". Love, understand one another and provide harmonious situations and it will all be good. There is a lot to learn from children.

(Daily Word ref. 25) " I find joy in observing children as they find delight in even the simplest aspects of life – the excitement of finding a bug in the garden, the fun of rolling in the grass, the joy of running in the rain. I am grateful for the love children and I have shared and for the wonderful adults they are becoming or have become."

This is exactly the way I feel about my children. Raising my children and enjoying them today as adults is the utmost satisfaction of my life. In the 1980's and early 90's we went to Disney from Wisconsin for vacation. When I look back now, however, I have to say that I enjoyed our 1st camping experience much more. We took a trip to Iowa and Missouri (Mark Twain country). If you have never read Huckleberry Finn, read it. It's about a boy and a slave searching for freedom. Great moral on how children can teach adults some lessons. All of Mark Twains stories and quotes make you think! My husband came up with the idea to rent a camper and go camping for a change. We had a truck camper in the yard for several years that the kids used as a playhouse and they always enjoyed that. We all had a great time. Campgrounds had everything we needed: playgrounds, pools, activities, movies, family togetherness, nature walks and the fresh outdoors of course. It was much more laid back (and no lines like at Disney). It was a vacation where you didn't come home and feel like you needed another vacation.

Try different things in life, don't keep doing the same old same old. I'm in my mid 50's and last year my daughter and I visited my son out in California. We went paragliding and jet skiing. Enjoy family time no matter what your age, you need to play.

(Bible ref. 25) Job 33:25 "Let him return to the days of his youthful vigor."

(Quote ref. 106) by Joyce Brothers: *"For many, the happiest times occur within the family."*

Share time, attention and ideas with loved ones. Always end prayers with: this or something better for all those concerned. This leaves the door open for the universe to surprise you with the unexpected. This is for the good of all, because everything gives us a chance for growth.

FAMILY: *"My Journal Time"* - I use to call family meetings when I thought things were out of sorts. Get together for venting feelings and solutions. What ways can you think of to ensure that everyone is being loved, understood, and comfortable? Do you expect perfection from yourself or others? If yes – how can you tone that down a bit? What fun things can you think of doing to get out of the same old same old? What can you do to bring more balance and harmony into everyday life?

My Journal

My Journal

My Journal

Chapter 26

Generations

It's sad to think that generations were more family orientated years ago. Somewhere along the line there was a huge melt-down of family values. Years ago people didn't move around so much like they do now. Families got together on weekends and had round robins on the holidays. Now, because of leaving hometowns for jobs or whatever, families are not together as much as they use to be. The structure of family has changed dramatically and it seems as though no one remembers or even knows what generations can actually do for the nucleus of a family.

Here is my breakdown of the word generations: (G) Giving and receiving of information and loving moral values. (E) Empathy or understanding of others. (N) Nourishing others in mind, body and soul. (E) Energy in all positive ways. (R) Remembering and finding compassion for things you went through. (A) Appreciating the differences of generations and learning from one another. (T) Teaching and learning ways to get along. (I) Inspiring others to live life to the fullest. (O) Options are always there for you. (N) Nostalgia is fine as long as you learn something positive from it. (S) Stories are what make the world go round. Other generations can help. Remember our purpose here is to serve one another.

GENERATIONS: *"My Journal Time"* – If you have family from several generations – how can you bring everyone closer for family get togethers? How about starting a family tree? If you don't have family – there are people in nursing homes that would love to spend time with you or your children. Also – family consists of people who are positive in your life – search and ye shall find!! How do you mingle with all age groups?

My Journal

My Journal

My Journal

Chapter 27

Health

Your health depends on the connection between your mind, body and soul. The key is to use preventative medicine to derail getting sick in the first place.

(Quote ref. 107) Thomas Edison: *"The doctor of the future will give no medicine, but will interest patients in the care of the human frame, in diet, and in the cause and prevention of disease."*

(Quote ref. 108) by Charles Dickens: *"Prevention is better than cure."*

(Quote ref. 109) by Hippocrates (Original father of medicine) (460 – 377 B.C.): *"A wise man should consider that health is the greatest of human blessings, and learn how by his own thought to derive benefit from his illnesses."*

(Quote ref. 110) by Hippocrates: *"Prayer indeed is good, but, while calling on the gods, a man should himself lend a hand."*

In other words – you don't sit there smoking a cigarette and pray you never have respiratory problems – not the way to go people. Take care of your selves.

(Daily Word ref. 26) "I am blessed with an unfailing ability to make healthful choices for myself. I have many opportunities to choose what supports my wholeness and wellbeing."

(Book ref. 24) The following was taken from: *"Your body can talk"* by Susan L. Levy "You can resolve the past, begin to create positive energy around you and reclaim the power over your miraculous mind-body. Begin your journey now with the recognition that sufficient self-esteem, along with the investment of your time, energy, and full range of emotions, may be the secret to maintaining good health on your mental and physical path to wellness."

(Book ref. 6) *"You can heal your life"* by Louise Hay: She explains the mind, body and soul connection. I started with simple preventative and alternative methods to better health. Acupressure, affirmations, visualization, mind, body and soul connections, good daily nutrition and exercise, are all good places to start. Also be sure that you work on any and all relationship issues.

(Daily Word ref. 27) "The cells of my body are working in concert together, assuring that I am whole, well, and free."

(Book ref. 25) *"Walk in Balance"* by Sun Bear, Crysalis Mulligan, Peter Nufer, and Wabun; "Defending your destiny is your given right and your responsibility. In order to be a spiritual warrior you must begin by cleaning up your own act, ridding yourself of the things that cause you pain and frustration. You need either to digest or disgorge the things that are eating at you, no matter how long they've been doing so. Preventative care on all levels of being is mandatory to well-being."

Water is the flow of life. Drink plenty of water and have the sound of water in your home. Get yourself a table water fountain. Your ears hear it, your eyes see it, it speaks to you as you meditate. You can also get cd's with water sounds, extremely relaxing to mind, body and soul. Before going to sleep, always do something relaxing. Read something positive and/ or listen to relaxing music. Read positive bedtime stories to your kids, and always give thanks for the blessings of each day.

(Daily Word ref. 28) "Nutritious foods and energizing exercise keep me aglow with vitality. My body moves with flexibility, balance, and fluidness. My mind is clear and I am alert. My very cells dance with exuberance. I am revitalized!"

Always ask about alternative methods that you don't understand. Work with your regular doctor on all health issues.

HEALTH: *"My Journal Time"*- List the preventative measures that you will take. Remember to list them by saying: "I am eating nutritional food or I am ridding toxic relationships from my life." Make a contract out with yourself that you are already doing something to take preventative measures and then – of course - do them!

My Journal

My Journal

My Journal

Chapter 28

Integrity / Interdependence

Integrity basically means that you are honest. You have high morals and you have sound values. You try to do everything with the utmost care and completeness. People that have integrity are usually people who are known for going that extra mile to help. Integrity is a very valuable asset and is obtained by those who are extremely humane. It is viewed as the highest character reference. Integrity is one of the universal words - see Chapter 2: Spirituality. "To thine own self be true."

Interdependence is also a character reference and it means that you are dependent and independent. It means that you can do things on your own but that your ego hasn't completely taken you over to make you out to be a complete ass. We all need to work together, interdependently. Both integrity and interdependence are assets to being of service to others.

(Quote ref. 111) Unknown quote: *"What the world needs is a declaration of interdependence."*

INTEGRITY/INTERDEPENDENCE – *"My Journal Time"* – Are you always honest – both with yourself and others? Do you do things with care and completeness? Do you work well alone and with others? List ways you can become interdependent and have integrity.

My Journal

My Journal

My Journal

Chapter 29

Journey

The journey consists of all the doors in your life. That's why you need to keep the door open at all times. It means a trip from one place to another (or one door to the next door). You're not on a journey if you're in a rut somewhere (you let the door close). You have to find the lesson in everything and keep moving, otherwise you're not on the journey anymore. We are all here to participate in the journey. Hop on the odyssey path for your spiritual quest. There are many choices, you just have to be aware of them when they are trying to get your attention.

(Daily Word ref. 29) "I put my own creative plans into motion, remaining open to God's guidance every step of the way."

(Daily Word ref. 30) "Divine appointments bring us together with wonderful companions to share our journeys. Wherever our journeys take us, we can trust that God is with us, guiding and protecting us along our way."

Pursuing and searching are required for the journey that you choose. If you don't keep pursuing, then your journey becomes a stand still venture, which gets you no where. The only time you should be at a stand still is when you get an obstacle, then of course you need to stop, look and listen. Even when you meditate and just be, you still have to listen and when you pray, you have to talk.

The journey isn't just the big journey of life, or finding your assignment. You have many little journeys. The journey of learning to walk, talk, and eat as a baby. The lessons of youth as a student in school and learning about self and relationships. The lessons of adulthood and parenthood. All your lessons are combined to bring you through the journey. That is why it is so important to learn lessons and go through them.

JOURNEY: *"My Journal Time"* – Are you keeping that door open? Are you moving on in your journey or are you stuck somewhere? You know what you need to do now -so just do it. Learn the lesson - and move on. Have you had any obstacles? Did you stop look and listen for the lesson? How about your dream journal, have your dreams been helping you solve obstacles and questions?

My Journal

_____
_____
_____
_____
_____
_____
_____
_____
_____
_____
_____
_____
_____
_____
_____
_____
_____
_____
_____
_____
_____
_____
_____
_____
_____
_____
_____
_____
_____
_____
_____

My Journal

My Journal

Chapter 30

Knowledge

Remember that even though knowledge is defined as awareness of facts, truths, or principles, many forget the awareness part in everyday situations. Remember what you read about wisdom. You have to be aware of everything and apply what you learn to everyday life. What good does it do to know something, if you're not going to put it into action in a positive way. Look at every situation and be sure that you aren't like one of those maps at a shopping mall marked you are here. Where do you want to go from that spot, right or left, or is where you want to go right in front of you? Be sure that you apply your knowledge in positive healthy ways.

(Quote ref. 112) by Albert Einstein: *"Imagination is more important than knowledge."*

(Quote ref. 113) by Sri Ramakrishna: *"Your knowledge becomes wisdom after putting it to work."*

But be sure you have awareness!!

KNOWLEDGE: *"My Journal Time"* – Are you using your knowledge in positive ways? how? Are you applying what you know and do you know where you're going? Remember, you can have plans, just don't get too caught up in all the details. Just because the universe has the last say, you still need to get on a path and keep your eyes on that door in case you have to change paths.

My Journal

My Journal

My Journal

Chapter 31

Kindness

I worked at a community college in the bookstore where I ran across a girl that was clearly on a non-productive path. Every time she came into the store she was angry. No one could please her. She cursed about everything and anything. We tried to please her in a kind way, but she continued her behavior. She needed a book that we didn't have in yet and we assured her that there would not be a problem in class. About a month passed and no one had seen hide nor hair of her. Then she came in one day on crutches and had a brace. She waited patiently in a long line and when she approached me she apologized for the way she had acted the previous month. She said that I was always kind to her and she was sorry. She approached the other staff members the same. She then announced that the last time she was here, she left and got in a terrible car accident. It was a total wake up call for her – and it changed her attitude on life. Pain made her think about her life. Then, and only then, she could begin to heal. Universe stopped her motion by making her be and see.

(Book ref. 6) *"You can heal your life"* by Louise Hay "Accidents are no accident. Like everything in our lives, we create them. Accidents are expressions of anger. We get so mad we want to hit people, and instead, we get hit." Pay particular attention if you get hurt somewhere. Louise says "Where this pain occurs in the body gives us a clue to which area of life we feel guilty about." In the case of the girl – it was her leg. When you look up (leg) in heal book - Louise says "Our legs carry us forward in life. Leg problems often indicate fear of moving or a reluctance to move forward in a certain direction."

Maybe it had something to do with what the girl was taking up in school. Maybe she was to change her attitude of life so she could continue moving in a more positive direction.

(Bible ref. 26) Colossians 3:14 "Above all, clothe yourselves with love, which binds everything together in perfect harmony."

Keep in mind that people are not attacking you personally and that what they say or do to you is a sign that they are hurting. Offer help, be kind, but if they are not ready for help, that is where you need to exercise your patience with their behavior. Be kind, but with in reason and with in your boundaries.

I'm sure you have all run across someone that has reached their limit or even have reached the limit yourself. It is times like those that your kindness is tested. Anyone can be kind to the kind but when you can reach out to someone that is hurting in some way and still be kind, you can bet that there is a lesson to be found in there somewhere. Show compassion and kindness to your fellow person, always try to help. Note: You can extend help but if the person is totally not willing to change their situation, then tell a professional about the situation. It falls under draining you if you are getting ill over it. That's the time to let go and let God.

(Quote ref. 114) by Ella Wheeler Wilcox: *"So many gods, so many creeds, So many paths that wind and wind, When just the art of being kind Is all this sad world needs."*

Kindness is one of the universal words – see Chapter 2: Spirituality.

(Quote ref. 115) unknown quote: *"Celebrate kindness: indulge in forgiveness. Life is too short to go sour."*

KINDNESS: *"My Journal Time"* – Have you been with some one who has reached their limit? Did you reach out and help? Why or why not? All people need to be treated with kindness – especially someone who is hurting. What ways can you extend kindness to your fellow person?

My Journal

My Journal

My Journal

Chapter 32

Love/Relationships

(Bible ref. 27) John 3:11 "For this is the message you have heard from the beginning, that we should love one another."

Love brings peace and positivity. Hate brings war and negativity.

(Bible ref. 28) Galatians 5:22-23 Fruit of the spirit: "But the fruit of the Spirit is love, joy, peace, patience, kindness, goodness, faithfulness, gentleness, self-control."

Love stands for (L) Loads, (O) Of, (V) Voiced, (E) Empathy. Love is one of the universal words – see Chapter 2: Spirituality. The key to love is to understand another, and this goes back to loads and loads of connecting with communication. Holding, hugging and cuddling are all forms of loving and we all enjoy the feeling we get when we engage in this contact. The (V) stands for voicing your feelings. What we need to do more of is say loving words, say I understand, say how can I help, say I love you. Really try to understand people and take time to talk and keep communication open. The (E) for empathy stands for understanding of another person. Putting yourself in their shoes. You share another persons feelings and help them by encouragement and giving of your time. Be sure that you keep communication lines open, and that you help but let others live their life.

There are toxic people out there, so keep your boundaries up. Remember your lessons and apply them to your relationships. There are, what I call: "kings and queens of mean" that are here to take advantage of people. Remember, these are your utmost grandest lessons of all!! There are snakes in the grass and wolves in sheeps clothing that come in the meanest forms imaginable. If you get one of these, it means the universe is at it's last straw with you. It means that you are truly being tested to learn your lesson and get it once and for all. The universe wants you to say, enough is enough!! Enough of abuse, of no respect and no appreciation. The universe and God do not want you to suffer, but if you're going to keep repeating things that do not benefit your mind, body and soul, the same lessons will be repeated, take my word for it!!

After you have said good bye to these kings and queens once and for all, you will truly be on the path to recovery of truly loving yourself. When you have gone through a lot of experiences you will be able to serve and help others.

(Quote ref. 116) by Lydia M. Child: *"The cure for all the ills and wrongs, the cares, the sorrows, and the crimes of humanity, all lie in the one word "love." It is the divine vitality that everywhere produces and restores life. To each and every one of us, it gives the power of working miracles."*

(Bible ref. 29) 1Corinthians 13:4-7 "Love is always patient and kind; it is never jealous. Love is never boastful or conceited; never rude or selfish. Love does not take offense, and is never resentful. Love takes no pleasure in other peoples sins, But delights in the truth. Love is always ready to excuse, to trust, to hope, and to endure whatever comes. Love does not come to an end."

(Lyric ref. 35) *"Imagine"* - "You may say I'm a dreamer, but I'm not the only one. I hope someday you'll join us, and the world will live as one"

An aunt and uncle of mine were married for 30 years. She made several meals that she thought my uncle liked (because he said he liked them). One day she overheard him tell someone he was sick and tired of a stew that had a million and one different ingredients in it. She approached him and asked him why he never told her he didn't like the stew. He said that he didn't want to hurt her feelings. She told him that he should have told her because she hated making that stew, it was tedious work cutting up all those ingredients. The only reason she made it, was because he told her he liked it. She was happy she didn't have to make it anymore, he was happy he didn't have to eat it anymore. They both thought they were pleasing each other, but found out 30 years later that they both disliked what they were doing.

If you break the above story down to days, it looks like this. Say she made the meal 2 times a month. That is 24 times per year times 30 years. Total of 720 days of saying (ho hum not this dam stew again (or) every time I make this stew I could say dammit. All because there was no communicating. There was maybe peace in the house but not in their souls.

(Quote ref. 117) by Nancy Lynn Martin (Author) " Don't be afraid to rock the boat. Rocking the boat is better than sinking the boat. Communicating (rocking) the boat – says (you care). Not communicating (sinking) the boat, says (you don't care) to keep the boat-(relationship)….afloat."

How else will you know the truth then getting it from the horses mouth? Don't assume a damm thing. Keep communication lines open.

Issues that are never resolved cause pent up frustrations which create a toxic environment. Don't let issues get out of hand to the point where thoughtless words come out that can leave lasting wounds that will be extremely hard to heal. Rocking the boat is not creating a conflict – it's resolving a conflict that has already surfaced.

Communication and understanding must be part of a relationship along with respect, patience, agreements, laughter, showing appreciation and giving of time. This goes for any relationship, friendship, acquaintance, people you talk to, pets, people from other lands, everybody. These parts of a relationship bring in positive forces so that things keep in balance and are harmonious.

(Lyrics ref. 36) *"What the world needs now is love sweet love"* - " What the world needs now, is love sweet love. It's the only thing that there's just too little of, No, not just for some, but for everyone."

 (Lyrics ref. 37) *"What a wonderful world"* - " I see friends shaking hands – Saying how do you do? They're really saying, I love you."

(Quote ref. 118) by Ursula K. Leguin: *"Love doesn't just sit there like a stone; it has to be made, like bread, remade all the time, made new."*

No one knows what you need better than yourself. Sometimes you hear someone say: "Well, if you really loved me, you would know

206

exactly what I need all the time." First of all, that's insane. No one but you can know exactly what you need all the time. Yes, people can be visual and see what pleases you, but not know everything. You can't expect that from anyone. Second of all, you are supposed to be whole yourself and not be in need of someone attending to your every beckon call. This goes for sex too. Spouse/lover not in the mood? So what. Get over it. Expect nothing from no one, that way you will be surprised when someone does please you in a loving manner. Love is always unconditional, remember?

(Quote ref. 119) Unknown quote: *"Calm someone, understand who they are and why."*

(Quote ref. 120)   by Joanne Woodward – Wife of Paul Newman: *"Sexiness wears thin after a while and beauty fades, but to be married to a man who makes you laugh every day, ah, now that's a real treat."*

LOVE: *"My Journal Time"* – Do you show appreciation, give your time, communicate, understand, respect, have patience, make out agreements and laugh in your relationships? If not, how will you in the future? When you do something for someone are you seeing the whole picture of the whole matter? If you had an experience like my aunt and uncle – have you learned something from it – and what can you do to avoid it from happening again?   Do you exercise unconditional love? Are you a demand sex person or a loving sex person?

My Journal

My Journal

My Journal

_____
_____
_____
_____
_____
_____
_____
_____
_____
_____
_____
_____
_____
_____
_____
_____
_____
_____
_____
_____
_____
_____
_____
_____
_____

Chapter 33

Music And All The Arts
Do The Dance Of Life In Every
Creative Pursuit

(Quote ref. 121) by Ludwig van Beethovan: *"Music is a higher revelation than all wisdom and philosophy. Music is the electrical soil in which the spirit lives, thinks and invents."*

(Quote ref. 122) by Plato: *"Music gives soul to the universe, wings to the mind, flight to the imagination and life to everything."*

(Quote ref. 123) by Henry David Thoreau: *"The world is but a canvas to the imagination."*

Listen to all different kinds of music. Many times you hear that someone is just into one type of music. They like just jazz, country, rock and roll, alternative, or whatever. This is putting limits on your growth. Sit and listen to different kinds of music in the music stores or take out cd's from the library. You can also listen to different stations on the radio or on the internet.

(Quote ref. 124) by Jane Ira Bloom: *"Sometimes I throw sound around the band like paint – other times I play and feel as if I was carving silence like a sculptor."*

Go to different kinds of concerts and different musicals. Always try to expand your listening pleasures, don't limit yourself. Each kind of music can put you in a different mood and take you to different levels that need to be explored. We need diversity in our music to balance us, just like an orchestra needs different instruments for different harmony and balance.

(Quote ref. 125) by Bono – U2: *"Music can change the world because it can change people."*

(Quote ref. 126) by J. Allen Boone: *"We are members of a vast cosmic orchestra, in which each living instrument is essential to the complementary and harmonious playing of the whole."*

(Quote ref. 127) by Agnes de Mille: *"The truest expression of a people is in its dances and its music. Bodies never lie."*

(Quote ref. 128) by Mata Hari: *"The dance is a poem of which each movement is a word."*

What ever part of the arts strikes your fancy, try your hand in it in any way shape or form that you can think of. Just like music – try all aspects of the art that you are interested in and add others for your creative pleasures and passions. If you like to paint, try all forms of it. If you like to bake or cook, try worldwide fare. Like to sew, try knitting, embroidery, applique. If you like to act, try comedy, drama etc. If you're into design work, try all avenues of designing. Never ever limit yourself in any of your creative talents. Don't say "I am a chef." Say " I am the maker of scrumptious world fare." Say " I am the maker of getting your thoughts in awe and tickle your fancy." (This can be said for an artist, musician, designer, writer, etc).

(Book ref. 26) *"Joy is my Compass"* by Alan Cohen "When we get fed up with feeling limited, we pop out of our shell of littleness and claim who we really are."

(Quote ref. 129) by Wynetka Ann Reynolds: *"If we are to contribute to a livable society, we must strive to assure that poetry exists to temper technology, that music enlivens and enhances our educational growth; that dance and sculpture challenge our imaginations as much as any new scientific discovery."*

(Quote ref. 130) by Twyla Tharp: *"Art is the only way to run away without leaving home."*

(Quote ref. 131) by Lucian Freud: *"What do I ask of a painting? I ask it to astonish, disturb, seduce, convince."*

(Quote ref. 132) by Star Riches: *"Art is when you hear a knocking from your soul and you answer."*

(Quote ref. 133) by Amy Lowell. *"Art is the desire of man to express himself, to record the reactions of his personality to the world he lives in."*

(Quote ref. 134) by John Updike: *"What art offers is space, a certain breathing room for the spirit."*

(Quote ref. 135) by Kenneth Tynan: *"No theater could sanely flourish until there was an umbilical connection between what was happening on the stage and what was happening in the world."*

(Quote ref. 136) by Stanley Kubrick: *"A film is - or should be – more like music than like fiction. It should be a progression of moods and feelings."*

Use your creativity in every way and please encourage fundings for all the arts.

MUSIC AND ALL THE ARTS: *"My Journal Time"* – List the types of music you like. Are there more than 3 kinds? If not – listen to different kinds. What do you do in the line of THE ARTS? Do you paint? Sculpt? Act? Compose? Cook? Design? How can you expand those creative talents? How do you express yourself? How do you support the ARTS?

My Journal

My Journal

My Journal

Chapter 34

Nature

(Quote ref. 137) by Thor Heyerdahl. *"Man is demolishing nature: we kill things that keep us alive."*

We need to watch nature more to see and hear how nature works. Everything in nature works with cycles. Watch the animals. They know what to do during each season.

(Book ref. 25) *"Walk in Balance"* by Sunbear "Nature is not dumb. Humanity is dumb when we can't hear or when we forget how to communicate with nature."

Nature is everything that is natural. Always try to use natural products.

(Book ref. 27) *"The Nontoxic Home and Office"* by Debra Lynn Dadd is an excellent earthwise consumer guide. Everything you need to know about alternatives to everyday toxins is covered in this highly informative book.

(Book ref. 28) *"Diet for a Poisoned Planet"* by David Steinman - an excellent resource book to choose safe foods and alternatives to chemicals. Be sure that you use recyclable products and that you recycle to save our landfills.

(Quote ref. 138) by Lorraine Anderson: *"Nature has been for me, as long as I can remember, a source of solace, inspiration, adventure, and delight; a home, a teacher, a companion."*

(Lyric ref. 38) There is a wonderful cd with nature sounds called *"Liquid Silk"*. Beautiful nature sounds and the native flute prove to be relaxing and rejuvenating.

(Quote ref. 139) by John Muir - Naturalist: *"I only went out for a walk and finally concluded to stay out till sundown, for going out, I found, was really going in."* He said of Yosemite - *"It is carved by glaciers, has mountains, waterfalls, and cliffs. It has giant sequoia trees. God himself seems to be doing his best here."* And also he said - *"By nature – you can best answer questions of life and it's meaning."*

NATURE: *"My Journal Time"* – What have you done lately where you got involved in nature? How do you help your environment? Do you recycle? What will you do to cut down on toxic chemicals? What are your feelings on organic foods?

My Journal

My Journal

My Journal

Chapter 35

Optimist/Pessimist

A well known saying: An optimist sees an opportunity in every calamity; a pessimist sees a calamity in every opportunity. Dolly Parton was featured in the July 2004 issue of the Guideposts Magazine. It stated she knows her greatest blessing is simply being a happy person.

(Quote ref. 140) *"A positive attitude and a sense of humor go together like biscuits and gravy."* She also stated that friends and family, work, laughter, prayer, and love add up to a joyful life.

(Quote ref. 141) by Frederick Langbridge: *"Two men look out through the same bars: One sees the mud, and one the stars."*

It's all up to you and your thoughts, your attitude. Only you can decide what kind of life you want. If you want to complain all the time, do so, but then don't wonder why your life is the way it is. It's your responsibility to make your life, you make the choices. Continue being a pessimist if you want, but don't complain to an optimist, because we will just tell you - God bless you and bye bye!!

(Lyrics ref. 39) *"His love is coming over me"* - "What's so wrong about daydreaming – what's so bad about being optimistic."

When you become buddies with the universe, you become more in tune with everything and you know what you have to do in a situation. You become aware that you need to go through something and not around it.

(Lyrics ref. 40) *"Strollin on the water"* - "Strollin on the water – high over every care. Strollin on the water – sinking no longer."

You become more joyful and have faith that everything will work out for the good of all concerned.

OPTIMIST/PESSSIMIST: *"My Journal Time"* – Which one are you? Why? Make a list of things that are positive to you and a list of negative things. Compare the 2 lists and see if you can come up for a reason for the differences between the two. How can you make it just one list, all on the positive side?

My Journal

My Journal

My Journal

Chapter 36

Peace

(Quote ref. 142) by Black Elk: *"Peace comes to the souls of human beings as they realize that they are one with the universe."*

Like I said before, become buddies with the universe. Everything is connected like a big puzzle. When you work together, things start to work. You do have to work on yourself however, to get to the point of how everything comes together. If you don't learn from all your lessons and apply those lessons to life, than of course you need to get on the right path again. Re-learn until you get it!

(Quote ref. 143) by Ralph Waldo Emerson: *"Nothing will bring you peace except yourself."* Also *" Peace cannot be achieved through violence, it can only be attained through understanding."*

(Quote ref. 144) by Maurice Maeterlinck: *"To have peace and confidence within our souls – these are the beliefs that make for happiness."*

Peace is one of the universal words – see Chapter 2: Spirituality.

(Quote ref. 145) by Edith Armstrong: *"I keep the telephone of my mind open to peace, harmony, health, love and abundance. Then, whenever doubt, anxiety or fear try to call me, they keep getting the busy signal – and they'll soon forget my number."*

(Daily Word ref. 31) from 2007 World Peace calendar "We bless the world with acceptance, understanding, and peace."

The Dalai Lama stands for peace, kindness, justice and inner strength.

(Quote ref. 146) Peace/War Poem

Peace and love serves all - war – what is it good for?

By Nancy Lynn Martin - Author

What a beautiful world we live in
How dare we complain
Be nice to friends - strangers and kin

There are magnificent mountains
And the Grand Canyon too
And don't forget the lion dens

How about the little bird nests
Or those little working ants
Not to mention the other little pests

We could learn a lot from an ant
They all work together
You never hear them rave and rant

Nature abounds us with mighty trees
Along with a bright warm sun
Learn to listen and understand people – geeze

Sun comes up in the morning- moon at night
Ocean tides even have a pattern
And ducks fly south when the time is right

People wake up before it's to late
Why do we try to fool others
And try to make them take the bait

Love conquers all
War is for fools
Wake up people before we fall

We now have guns instead of clubs
We haven't progressed since the caveman
We just went from clubs to slugs

Some come back from war and will never walk
And some come back in a box
All because man can't negotiate and talk

Are we back in the garden of Eden
Blame Blame Blame
Didn't we learn that was wrong in kindergarten

Love is the answer my dears
Let us fight no more
What is it that man fears

Have we gone back in time
Fighting like cowboys and Indians
All for the sake of a dime

We should be doing things that bring love
And live for Gods' glory
Use our gifts that came from above

There are little and big creatures – oh my
Endless grass, deserts and air to breathe
And what about the beautiful sky

Oceans that run deep
Roads that run wide
What man sows - he will reap

It's a wonderful world we live in
Learn to understand and get along
Have some empathy so we all win

(Bible ref. 30) John 14: 27 " Peace I leave with you, My peace I give to you; not as the world gives do I give to you. Let not your heart be troubled, neither let it be afraid."

PEACE: *"My Journal Time"* – How are you coming along with becoming buddies with the universe? List the ways that you are working at "getting it." What are your views of war and why? How are you working at peaceful situations in your life? What are your views on world peace?

My Journal

My Journal

My Journal

Chapter 37

Perseverance

(Quote ref. 147) by Calvin Coolidge: *"Nothing in the world can take the place of persistence. Talent will not; nothing is more common than unsuccessful men with talent – Genius will not; unrewarded genius is almost a proverb. Education alone will not; the world is full of educated derelicts. Persistence and determination alone are omnipotent."*

When you have great passion for something, no naysayer can stop you from attaining your dream. Believe in yourself.

(Bible ref. 25) Hebrews 3:14 "For we have become partakers of Christ if we hold the beginning of confidence steadfast to the end."

Perseverance is like setting boundaries. It takes a lot of discipline. You will be doing things differently which is hard to do sometimes, especially when you were in a comfort zone. When, however, you are at the point of saying enough is enough and you know you need to change, heal, and grow, than the student (you) will be ready.

When you're on your spiritual journey, you can't just do spiritual work once in a while. Be determined to "get it" now and all of a sudden you will have an Aha! moment. You will reap rewards when you have gone through everything you need to do- to get where you are supposed to be. You will reap peace of mind and inner strength with each experience and lesson that has been planted. Do what you have to do and know that you are being prepared for your greater good and for the good of all concerned.

(Bible ref. 32) Habakkuk 3:19 "The Lord God is my strength; He will make my feet like deer's feet, And He will make me walk on my high hills."

Years ago there was a bumper sticker that said "Keep on Truckin." I'm adding to that "don't forget to change the load." You need to persevere by making changes. You can't get different results if you don't change. Your load includes your choices. God wants us to heal and grow but he will not interfere with our choices. God cannot save you until you are ready. You receive what you need, information and the experiences, but you really save yourself by following through.

(Lyrics ref. 41) *"Stomp"* - "Lately I've been goin' through some things thats really got me down. I need someone somebody to come and help me turn my life around. I can't explain it. I can't obtain it. Jesus your love is, it's so amazin. It gets me high, up to the sky."

(Bible ref. 33) Galatians 6:9-10 "And let us not grow weary while doing good, for in due season we shall reap if we do not lose heart. Therefore, as we have opportunity, let us do good to all, especially to those who are of the household of faith."

(Quote ref. 148) by Longfellow: *"Perseverance is a great element of success. If you only knock long enough and loud enough at the gate, you are sure to wake somebody up."*

(Quote ref. 149) by Albert Schweitzer: *"Do not lose heart even if you must wait a bit before finding the right thing. Be prepared for disappointment, also! But do not abandon the quest."*

PERSEVERANCE: *"My Journal Time"* - How are you working on getting it? What are you doing to change your load? How will you discipline yourself to change your life around once and for all?

My Journal

My Journal

My Journal

Chapter 38

Prayer
Speaking To God

Prayer is *speaking* to God whereas meditation is *listening* for God. See more on meditation in the zen section at end of book. Pray in the way that makes you most comfortable and in a way that is comforting to you. If you recite prayers you find, and are comforted, than do that. If you just start talking to God and are comforted, than do that. There is no right or wrong way to pray.

If you read prayers from a book or any types of readings, be sure they are prayers that have meaning to you. If you are just reading and the words aren't heartfelt, than choose words that are, or pray directly from self. You can be intimate with God by walking in nature, dancing, singing, creating, serving others, reading and having solitude time.

(Bible ref. 34) Matthew 21:22: "And whatever things you ask in prayer, believing, you will receive."

(Bible ref. 35) 1Timothy 2:1: "Therefore I exhort first of all that supplications, prayers, intercessions, and giving of thanks be made for all men."

(Lyrics ref. 42) *"What a friend we have in Jesus"* - "Oh, what peace we often forfeit, Oh, what needless pain we bear, All because we do not carry everything to God in prayer."

(Daily Word ref. 32) "Affirmative prayers are powerful statements of spiritual truth. They are faith-filled acceptance of my good even before it is evident to me."

Your prayer is always answered, just not the way you expect it to be answered. You get what you need to answer your prayer. It's up to you to figure out (seek) what to do with what you are given. Remember to ask, seek, and then knock and more doors will open!! When you pray, you get what you need, stepping stones.

(Lyrics ref. 43) *"Nothing Compares"* - "Nothing compares to the greatness of knowing you, Lord. I see all the people, wasting all their time building up their riches, for a life thats fine. I find myself just livin for today cause I don't know what tomorrows gonna bring."

When you pray and say (I want), you are really just making a statement. You're just stating a fact. The universe already knows long before you said it. You are not trusting the universe and the divine order. Sometimes you actually get this (want) that you asked for. The universe gives you what you want to see what you're going to do with it. Sometimes the lesson is that you find out you really didn't (want) something after all.

PRAYER: *"My Journal Time"* – Pray in the way that you are comforted. Use these pages for prayers that that are comforting to you.

My Journal

My Journal

My Journal

Chapter 39

QUESTIONS…..ASK THEM!!!!!!!

QUESTIONS: *"My Journal Time"* – Any questions? Ask them!! Then seek the answers.

My Journal

My Journal

My Journal

Chapter 40

Reasons/Seasons

(Book ref. 2) *"All the Joy you can Stand"* by Debra Jackson Gandy "One of the reasons that life occurs as hard and effort-full for many of us is that we fail to recognize that life has continuous cycles and seasons. When things fall into place effortlessly – the joy begins and you know you're on the right path."

Just like in nature, everything cooperates with the seasons. Animals know just what to do and the season to do it. Plants pull back for the fall and winter and push up for the spring and summer. See, we could learn a lot from watching and being aware of nature. Leaves fall off trees in the fall and start budding again in the spring. If nature knows what to do, than us humans certainly should figure it out, don't you think? Again, how does that make you feeeeeeeeeeeeeeeel? Doesn't that want you to persevere and figure out this buddies with the universe and "get it" once and for all?

"Sun comes up in the morning, moon comes out at night. Ocean tides even have a pattern and ducks fly south when the time is right." From my poem in Peace section.

Be aware of everything and get it through to yourself that everything happens for a reason. It is your responsibility to find out the reasons for everything that you encounter every day of your life. Some people are in your life that don't stick around forever, sometimes someone stays for a reason till you figure out the purpose. Other people stay for a season and stick around a little longer to teach you more, or you teach them. Some people stay around for your lifetime.

(Quote ref. 150) Following is from many sources, and it is called People:

"PEOPLE .....

....come into your life for a reason, a season, or a lifetime.
When you figure out which it is,
you know exactly what to do.

When someone is in your life for a reason,
it is usually to meet a need you have expressed
outwardly or inwardly.

They have come to assist you through a difficulty
to provide you with guidance and support,
to aid you physically, emotionally, or spiritually.

They may seem like a godsend, and they are.
They are here for the reason you need them to be.

Then, without any wrongdoing on your part
or at an inconvenient time, this person will say
or do something to bring the relationship to an end.

Sometimes they die.
Sometimes they walk away.
Sometimes they act up or out
and force you to take a stand.

What we must realize is that our need has been met,
and our desire fulfilled; their work is done.

The prayer you sent up has been answered
and it is now time to move on.

When people come into your life for a season,
it is because your turn has come to share, grow, or learn.

They may bring you an experience of peace or make you laugh.

They may teach you something you have never done.

They usually give you an unbelievable amount of joy.

Believe it! It is real! But, only for a season.

Lifetime relationships teach you lifetime lessons;
those things you must build upon in order to have
a solid emotional foundation.

Your job is to accept the lesson, love the person;
and put what you have learned to use in all other
relationships and areas of your life.

It is said that love is blind but friendship has a special sense."

(Quote ref. 151) Unknown quote: *"Do you sense a pattern? Do you feel
the interlocking harmonies dancing within? Every moment has a reason."*

(Bible ref. 36) Isaiah 40:31 "But those who wait on the Lord – Shall
renew their strength; They shall mount up with wings like eagles, They
shall run and not be weary, They shall walk and not faint."

There is a reason to wait – the season will come. You are being prepared
for renewal when the season is right.

(Daily Word ref. 33) "Life events unfold to create a collage of possibility
and wonder. We meet people and experience events that touch our lives
and cause our paths to wind in a new and more fulfilling direction.":

REASONS SEASONS: *"My Journal Time"* – What have you gone
through recently that you realized followed a cycle? What will you
do to let go and let God when you realize something is not working?
How do you feel about the poem, People? When you look back on
relationships do you see the connections to the terms, reason, season,
lifetime?

My Journal

My Journal

My Journal

Chapter 41

Soul

Reach deep into your soul and find what makes you completely lose track of time. What makes you feel alive? That's your passion. Maybe you lose time helping people, working with children, tinkering with electronics, reading, teaching, working on cars, doing something pertaining to the arts, driving. What ever it is be sure that your job contains an aspect of that passion. Take care of self, others, and time, by doing what you love and encourage others with their inspiration.

(Quote ref.152) by Thomas Moore: *"Everyone should know that you can't live in any other way than by cultivating the soul."*

You should also be an ageless soul. You need to keep replenishing your soul by following your passion, being creative, resting, and meditating. Balance is what keeps life spicy and interesting. Be a being and a doer. Take time to listen for guidance through inspiring ideas, dreams, and by being aware of all lessons.

(Quote ref. 153) by Erik Erikson: *"It is necessary for you to re-encounter the soul of the child within you."*

There's a story about a man who goes to medical school. At graduation, he hands his diploma to his parents and says "I believe this belongs to you. Now I am going to become a fireman like I told you since I was 6." Don't " give in" to another. Do what brings you joy. Don't let anyone steal your passion.

(Quote ref. 154) by Johann Wolfgang Goethe: *"As soon as you trust yourself you will know how to live."*

(Book ref. 29) *"The Man who Listens to Horses"* by Monty Roberts - Story of Monty who wrote in a school essay that he wanted his own thoroughbred racehorse facility. The assignment was to write an essay of your life in the future, as if all your ambitions had been realized. This was a deep passion, deep in Montys Soul since he was 9. His teacher gave him an F and told him that his dream was an unattainable dream because he knew his family and background and the teacher didn't see that type of a future for him - (the teacher was what I call a soul stealer - naysayer). Monty was given a chance to re-write the paper. Monty wasn't interested in a better grade, he was interested in keeping his dream. His farm in Solvang, California is called Flag Is Up Farms - his dream came true. Many years later the teacher came to the ranch and said he learned a lesson from Monty, his aspiration was attainable. (Monty is an inspirational man who has a nonverbal gentle communication with horses, an understanding that applies to human relations as well). This is just one of many stories of someone not giving up their dream. Don't ever let anyone talk you out of your dream, your dream is your true calling. Naysayers are soul stealers – weed them out!! Your soul is not for sale!

(Quote ref. 155) by Annie Besant: *"No soul that aspires can ever fail to rise; no heart that loves can ever be abandoned. Difficulties exist only that in overcoming them we may grow strong."*

When I was a young girl I played with dolls, played house, library, played store with parents record albums and played school. I also sold crafts that I made door-to-door. Mid-20's to now, I love being a mom. If I could set up a cot at a library, I would. I'm always reading. I love music. Look forward to starting an inspirational shop. I thought of being a teacher, but I don't agree with the educational system so I worked in lots of different places and talked with tons of people and I hope I have put some positivity in their lives. I am writing this book to help motivate others to live a fulfilling life. What I loved as a child, I am doing with my life now, some in quite unexpected ways, I might add, but that's the universe for you, always surprising us!

(Quote ref. 156) by Thoreau: *"If one advances confidently in the direction of his dreams, he will meet a success unexpected in common hours."*

(Quote ref. 157) by Mencius: *"The great man is one who does not lose his childlike nature."*

(Bible ref. 37)   Psalm 1:2-3 (the well nourished soul – the way of the righteous) " But his delight is in the law of the Lord, And in His law he meditates day and night. He shall be like a tree – Planted by the rivers of water, That brings forth its fruit in its season. Whose leaf also will not wither; And whatever he does shall prosper."

(Quote ref. 158) by Michelangelo: *"I saw the angel in the marble and I carved until I set him free."*

(Quote ref. 159) by Francoise de Motteville: *"The true way to render ourselves happy is to love our duty and find in it our pleasure."*

(Quote ref. 160) by Swami Sivananada: *"The peaceful state of one's soul is the most precious possession."*

(Lyrics ref. 44) *"What your soul sings"* - "Your mind can never change, unless you ask it to. Lovingly re-arrange the thoughts that make you blue. The things that bring you down, will mean no harm to you. And so make your choice joy. The joy belongs to you."

(Quote ref. 161) by Goethe: *"What has not burst forth from your own soul will never refresh you."*

(Daily Word ref. 34) "My life is a journey, a journey of the soul that uplifts me and leads me to the mountaintop experiences of life."

SOUL: *"My Journal Time"* – What makes you lose track of time? Are you living your passion, or at least making your way through the stepping stones to get there? Are you having second thoughts about your dream because of Naysayers? If yes, why? List everything you enjoyed as a child. Are you doing them now in one way or another? If not, why not?

My Journal

_____

_____

_____

_____

_____

_____

_____

_____

_____

_____

_____

_____

_____

_____

_____

_____

_____

_____

_____

_____

_____

_____

_____

_____

_____

My Journal

My Journal

Chapter 42

Past The 3 R's On To The 3 S's
Spirituality-Simplicity-Solitude

As I wrote before, spirituality pertains to the soul or spirit. It generates kindness, love, understanding, peace, integrity. It is the universal window both individually and globally. Spirituality is a partnership with God or your soul power. Spirituality is the construction of your mind, body and soul along with God. It's a progressive development that will take you all the way to the time that you will be able to say (I have done everything You have made me for – now I am home).

(Daily Word ref. 35) "To develop true spiritual freedom, I turn to God in prayer, and then I practice bringing my spiritual awareness into daily life."

When you live simple, you don't have all of the complexities that go along with having or doing too much. How much do you really need and does it all make you happy? Are you like the woman I wrote about that had her nails done because of others? What you need to do is eliminate confusion by knowing what makes you happy and balancing everything in the best way you know how to and keep it as simple as possible. When you rid the clutter of your mind and home – than you will really be living. We need to get back to the basics of life.

(Quote ref. 162) by Laura Ingalls Wilder: *"It is the sweet simple things of life which are the real ones after all."*

Always stop, look and listen. Taking pampered solitude time even for a half hour a day can do wonders for your mind, body and soul. Relax, re-new and meditate.

(Quote ref. 163) by William Penn: *"True silence is the rest of the mind, and it is to the spirit what sleep is to the body, nourishment and refreshment."*

(Quote ref. 164) by Paramahansa Yogananda: *"Be alone once in a while, and remain more in silence."*

3S'S: *"My Journal Time"* - How have you practiced the 5 universal words kindness, love, understanding, peace and integrity? How have you put simplicity into your life? List the ways that you are relaxing. As you meditate, what are you hearing?

My Journal

My Journal

My Journal

Chapter 43

They Say

They say, is a coined term which basically is a term used to dodge responsibility. If you say " You know what they say" - than you're not taking any responsibility for what you said. You're passing it off as they have said it. Years ago people would say "What will the neighbors say?" When it was decided by (who knows) that real people shouldn't be put as the bad guy, the term (they say) was formed. Then when kids caught on to the (imaginary blame syndrome) they started saying (not me) when they broke something. When I was about 6, I said to my mom "Show me these people called they, I want to meet them. What do they look like and what do they like to play with?" She of course was speechless. I figured I knew what my imaginary friends looked like, I knew what they liked to play with, I even knew where they lived. Certainly an adult should know these things, but no one had an answer.

THEY SAY: *"My Journal Time"* – Do you use the term they say? If yes, why don't you want to take responsibility for what you say?

My Journal

My Journal

My Journal

Chapter 44

Time

(Quote ref. 165)   Unknown quote: *"Her little girl was late arriving home from school so the mother began to scold her daughter but stopped and asked, "Why are you so late?" "I had to help another girl. She was in trouble," replied the daughter. "What did you do to help her?" "Oh, I sat down and helped her cry." Sometimes the best gift you can give someone is the gift of your time.*

(Lyrics ref. 45)   *"Fly like an Eagle"* - "Time keeps on slippin, slippin, slippin into the future. Fly like an eagle."

Don't let time slip away – don't say later – don't say some day. Time falls into the make every moment count.   Keep your creative juices flowing and your passions alive and fly!

(Quote ref. 166) by Lydia H. Sigourney: *"Lost – yesterday – somewhere between sunrise and sunset – two golden hours – each set with sixty diamond minutes. No reward is offered – for they are lost forever."*

Always be flexible to allow the unexpected that is sure to happen. If you stick to a strict routine or plan, you will miss an opportunity. Spend time seeking what you need to learn so that you can grow. The universe always sends us something or someone just at the right time. It's good to keep boundaries up, but this just like anything else, needs to be balanced so you can see new possibilities. What ever happens in your life, life goes on and time goes on. Again, make every moment count, be flexible and look for messages in the unexpected.

My daughter Jenny gave me a mothers day card one year that had a wristwatch on it. It said " Thanx for the time you freely give." My son Jake wrote several notes throughout the years writing "Thanks for always being there for me." It's a good feeling knowing that my time

268

has been so appreciated by them. Thank you Jen and Jake, and God bless you.

TIME: *"My Journal Time"* - Do you say someday? What ways are you preparing for your dreams to become reality? Remember, the universe has the last word but if you are not learning your lessons – you are limiting yourself from your true assignment. Life is work and a game, and yes there are some rules. Have you given somebody the gift of time today? How? Did you do something today out of your routine? What did you notice? If something negative happened because you went off the beaten path – did you learn the lesson ?

My Journal

My Journal

My Journal

Chapter 45

Understanding

(Book ref. 11) *"Wouldn't take nothing for my Journey now"* by Maya Angelou (Passports to understanding) "Perhaps travel cannot prevent bigotry, but by demonstrating that all peoples cry, laugh, eat, worry, and die, it can introduce the idea that if we try to understand each other, we may even become friends."

Understanding is one of the universal words, see Chapter 2: Spirituality.

(Quote ref. 167) by Carl Jung: *"We need more understanding of human nature, because the only real danger that exists is man himself."*

(Quote ref. 168) by Edgar Cayce: *"Know this: that what ever situation you find yourself in, it is what is necessary for your development. An entity must apply in its associations from day to day a word here and a word there, one today, another tomorrow and the next day, with the understanding that from that such activities in word, deed, self development will come. When an entity has prepared itself through constant forward movement towards service, the necessary circumstances for change will come about so that he may see the next step, the next opportunity... Haste not and be not over-anxious; for is not the whole of the building of His making?"*

Always try to understand one another and realize that we are all here to learn all of our individual lessons. Spend more energy on understanding situations and people instead of complaining about them.

(Quote ref. 169) by Indian proverb: *"I had no shoes and complained, until I met a man who had no feet."*

(Bible ref. 38) Proverbs 19:8 "He who gets wisdom loves his own soul; He who keeps understanding will find good."

There needs to be a better understanding of man and woman issues. Men need to search with-in and find their feminine side, which is hard to do because they have been the warrior for so long. There is a cd called Honorable Sky by Peter Kater and R. Carlos Nakai.

(Lyrics ref. 46) That has wonderful go-with-in music. R. Carlos Nakai has these inspiring words. "Our story is in the music of our feminine expressions that serve to balance our male ego and force, the controls that diminish or suppress our very being as feeling, loving human people."

Our young boys need to be taught that it is okay to show their feelings and express them instead of holding issues inside and then letting loose in dysfunctional ways. Women need to search with-in to find their masculine side, which is also hard to do because they have been considered the weaker sex for so long. We have the power to change the dysfunctional world we live in. Now more than ever (because of the percent of baby boomers over 50) we can change the world. Many changes are needed, violence has never worked, it's time to stop. Our young girls need to be taught that they have the power to change the world to be peaceful. By men keying into their more gentle nature and women keying into a more powerful nature, we can find a balance to live in harmony.

(Book ref. 30) "*Tao Teh Ching*" by Lao Tzu "To return to the root is to find peace. To fulfill one's destiny is to be constant. If one does not know the Constant, One runs blindly into disasters. If one knows the Constant, One can understand and embrace all. Tackle things before they have appeared. Cultivate peace and order before confusion and disorder have set in."

UNDERSTANDING: *"My Journal Time"* - In what ways are you trying to understand others more? Did you try walking in someones shoes today? How will you work on balancing male and female sides?

My Journal

My Journal

My Journal

Chapter 46

Vision Quest
Angel And Child Messengers

(Quote ref. 170) by Stephen Samuel Wise: *"Vision looks inwards and becomes duty. Vision looks outwards and becomes aspiration. Vision looks upwards and becomes faith."*

Your inner child is the door to your talent. Go inside and visualize yourself as a child again. Your inner child still holds your aspirations, your passions. Put aside time to give all your attention to your passion. This is a good activity to do before going to bed. Always have pen and paper ready to write down creativity ideas that usually pop in. Close your eyes, mentally envision a road ahead. As you are on the road, pay attention to the road signs, meander off exits once in a while to see what other roads have for you. Put the brakes on often so you can stop, look, and listen. Where did the road take you? Enter the Journey in my journal time.

(Daily Word ref. 36) Inner Vision by Norman V. Olsson (last 4 lines) "And we, like wildflowers no less, possess our own uniqueness; so dream the splendor and the sum – of all you may yet become!"

(Quote ref. 171) by Sylvia Browne: *"So much has failed humanity that the world has turned to a higher spiritual belief, a gentler belief. And what could be more gentler than an angel."*

(Quote ref. 172) by The Talmud: *"Every blade of grass has its own angel that bends over and whispers, grow – grow."*

(Quote ref. 173) Irish Blessing: *"May God grant you always – A sun beam to warm you – a moon beam to charm you – a sheltering angel so nothing can harm you. Laughter to cheer you. Faithful friends near you. And when ever you pray -heaven to hear you."*

(Quote ref. 174) by Unknown: *"Angels help us spread our wings and fly."*

(Quote ref. 175) by Unknown: *"Angels come in all shapes and sizes and colors."*

(Daily Word ref. 37) " Thank you, God, for children- Your vision of greater good in the world. I bless these wonderful miracles in my life, children who are my teachers, my reminders that each moment can be a new beginning."

Go on a vision quest and see what it would be like to give the gift of self. Give people attention, time, communication, peace, harmony, love, joy, understanding, patience, kindness, integrity. Give your presence, not presents!!

(Quote ref. 176) by John Wesley: *"Do all the good you can. By all the means you can. In all the ways you can. In all the places you can. At all the times you can. To all the people you can. As long as you ever can."*

(Lyrics ref. 47) *"Amazing Grace"* - "Amazing grace – how sweet the sound, that saved a wretch like me! I once was lost, but now am found, was blind, but now I see."

(Book ref. 31) *"In the Meantime"* by Ivanla Vanzant "Once you find love, true self love, and unconditional love for everyone all the time, things will look, feel, and be a lot better. What do you do in the mean time? - clean windows. In the mean time you know where you want to be – but you have no clue how to get there." - "Perhaps your vision is unclean, your purpose still undefined."

In her book – Ivanla says you have to do a lot of mental housekeeping so you have better vision of your life. She goes through the stages of renewal by using the floors of a house as the lessons. Very good reading and extremely interesting. From the *basement* figuring out where you need to heal-working through stuff to the *attic* which is love.

(Daily Word ref. 38) "As Spirit within illumines my mind, I am prayerfully guided. My inner vision is strengthened as I reflect upon choices of what to say and do."

VISION: *"My Journal Time"* - When you visit your inner child – what do you remember? Are you doing things that brought joy to you as a child? If not, why not? Where did the road vision meditation take you? Do you feel angels around you, nudging you along with their wings? Did you give your presence today? How? We are almost at the end of life door. How do you feeeeeeeel? Have you found your assignment, yourself? Do you see more clearly what you need to do with what you were given? How are you working on cleaning up your attic (your mind)? Are your thoughts going forward (positive) or are you in reverse (negative) on this ride of and for your life? How are you going to change?

My Journal

My Journal

My Journal

Chapter 47

War

Re-read school and rights section about war. An eye awakening article called "The Little White Lie" by Sharon Pacione is summarized below.

(Quote ref. 177) can be read in its entirety at www.sapphyr.net in the Native American wisdom section. *"It's time to wake up! War or peace, it's up to you. It is through awareness and understanding that humanity can purify the individual and collective hearts and minds, necessary components to bring about peace on this planet. The great purification spoken about in Native American prophecy can be as kind and gentle as humanity wishes it to be. We can either wake up and do the internal work ourselves, manifesting peace, or continue harboring fear and anger, manifesting war. It's as simple as that, and it's our choice! It is our actions (or lack of them) that are determining this very minute the type of world in which we choose to live."*

(Quote ref. 178) by Bertrand Russell: *"War does not determine who is right, only who is left."*

WAR: *"My Journal Time"* – Write your comments on the above article.

My Journal

My Journal

My Journal

Chapter 48

X-Tra
Words To Grow On

A LITTLE SOMETHING (X -TRA) A CROSSWORD PUZZLE

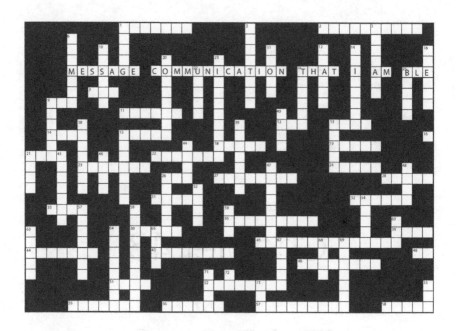

Crossword grid with filled letters spelling: MESSAGE COMMUNICATION THAT I AM BLE

ACROSS:

1) Become ___ with the universe
2) Put up___ to rid negativity
3) Honesty ___
4) Everything in nature is ___
5) Get along and come to ___ments
6) Different yet the same ___
7) Don't wait /start right ___
8) ___ Seek knock
9) Might not be your ___
10) Words to songs ___
11) Go after with intent ___
12) Tiny insect smarter than us ___
13) ___ Body and soul
14) Opposite of human being/ ___
15) Body movement that never lies ___
16) Compassion and understanding ___
17) Mind body and ___
18) 1st the ___ then the lessons
19) Gain wisdom and ___ with others
20) ___ is not dumb/humanity is

21) Give your ___ and your presence
22) It's the ___ not the destination
23) Hold on to passion/ be a ___
24) ___every mountain
25) One of the universal words ___
26) You reap what you ___
27) Reaches limit/ you extend___
28) Everything is based on our___
29) Another word for weed out ___
30) Support fundings for the ___
31) Become complete or ___
32) Group of things/people ___
33) ___ is this now
34) Alice & Dorothy had one
35) What you do with a book ___
36) Word for roadblocks
37) Having a partnership with
    God and pertains to your soul
38) Grownups are afraid to be ___
39) Give back to ___ what you take
40) Once and for all ___ (2words)

41) Your life is your ___
42) Embrace someone ___
43) ___Look and listen
44) Delete or ___ (2words)
45) Positive person ___
46) Your assignment or your ___
47) Surprised with the___
48) Be able to express our ___
49) Red flag/voice___ (2words)
50) We ___what we sow
51) We always get what we ___
52) Opposite of negative ___
53) End of each chapter/MY___
54) What we never stop doing___
55) ___Mind body and soul
56) Live in the now/ in the___
57) What you need to climb___
58) Find your talent – serve the people
    and then ___will come
59) Rest/ relax/___
60) ___ getting sick in the 1st place
61) You are not guaranteed___

290

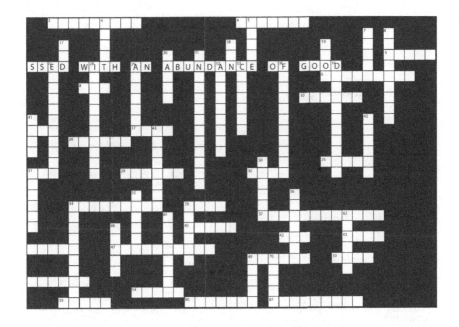

The crossword grid contains the partially filled answer: S S E D · W I T H · A N · A B U N D A N C E · O F · G O O D

DOWN:

1) Opposite of human doer ____
2) We all have a ____ talent
3) ____ Know what to do/season
4) ____ but not what they wanted
5) We all need solitude or ____ time
6) Word for in balance ____
7) ____ is the flow of life
8) Word for thankful ____
9) Act/ awareness of knowledge ____
10) Mental housekeeping/ clearer ____
11) Ask /Seek ____
12) ____ reaction = different effect
13) ____ and all the arts
14) ____ teach you to explain
15) Beat of a different ____
16) Don't let anyone steal your ____
17) Our CREATOR ____
18) Gravel/bench/ empty spaces ____
19) Eat nutritional ____
20) We all need alone time or ____
21) What is ____ now
22) Daily Word/Silent ____
23) No confusion/ basics ____
24) Find your God given ____

25) I have 34 references of ____
26) Educational establishment ____
27) Life is a series of ____
28) Encourage this in others ____
29) Be an ____ soul
30) Gain the ____ of a mustard seed
31) Better ____ man/woman
32) ____ Co-exists with wisdom
33) We have ____ and free will
34) ____ good deeds of others
35) Chapter 8 School/ ____
36) ____ rids negative energy
37) Right timing/ ____
38) ____ from limitation
39) Tests teach ____
40) Take different road/ ____
41) Rock the ____
42) Talking to God through ____
43) Buddies with the ____
44) To live is to ____
45) Someone elses shoes ____
46) No freedom ____ ringing
47) Listen for God ____
48) Mind ____ and soul

49) Better than good ____
50) Arts and ____
51) Preventative medicine for ____
52) ____ old wounds
53) Other word for happiness ____
54) ____ and child messengers
55) Put ____ pieces together
56) That which is given ____
57) Go ____ not around
58) Here to find our ____
59) Be your own ____ on wheel
60) ____ is to forgive
61) Name of this book ____
62) Stop look and ____
63) You have the ____
64) Other word for wait ____
65) Stop ____ and listen
66) One of the 3 L's ____
67) Here to ____ others
68) Ask ____ and knock
69) Build ____ not walls
70) Integrity is telling the ____
71) Always keep the door ____
72) What ____ this now
73) Start of an affirmation (2words)

291

ANSWERS TO CROSSWORD

ACROSS:

1) BUDDIES
2) BOUNDARIES
3) INTEGRITY
4) NATURAL
5) AGREE
6) DIVERSITY
7) NOW
8) ASK
9) WAY
10) LYRICS
11) PURSUE
12) ANT
13) MIND
14) DOER
15) DANCE
16) LOVE
17) SOUL
18) TESTS
19) SHARE
20) NATURE
21) TIME
22) JOURNEY
23) DREAMER
24) CLIMB
25) PEACE
26) SOW
27) KINDNESS
28) THOUGHTS
29) DELETE
30) ARTS

31) WHOLE
32) FAMILY
33) WHAT
34) ADVENTURE
35) READ
36) OBSTACLES
37) SPIRITUALITY
38) SILLY
39) EARTH
40) GETIT)
41) RESPONSIBILITY
42) HUG
43) STOP
44) WEEDOUT
45) OPTIMIST
46) PURPOSE
47) UNEXPECTED
48) FEELINGS
49) GUTLAW
50) REAP
51) NEED
52) POSITIVE
53) JOURNAL
54) LEARN
55) CONNECT
56) MOMENT
57) MOUNTAINS
58) MONEY
59) RENEW
60) PREVENT
61) HAPPINESS

DOWN:

1) BEING
2) CREATIVE
3) ANIMALS
4) RIGHT
5) ALONE
6) HARMONY
7) WATER
8) GRATITUDE
9) WISDOM
10) VISION
11) KNOCK
12) CHANGE
13) MUSIC
14) CHILDREN
15) DRUMMER
16) DREAMS
17) GOD
18) ZEN
19) FOOD
20) SOLITUDE
21) THIS
22) UNITY
23) SIMPLICITY
24) TALENT
25) BOOKS
26) SCHOOL
27) EXPERIENCES
28) INSPIRATION
29) AGELESS
30) FAITH
31) UNDERSTANDING
32) AWARENESS
33) CHOICES
34) APPRECIATE
35) RIGHTS
36) FORGIVENESS

37) DIVINEORDER
38) FREEDOM
39) LESSONS
40) PATH
41) BOAT
42) PRAYER
43) UNIVERSE
44) GROW
45) EMPATHY
46) BELL
47) MEDITATE
48) BODY
49) GREAT
50) CRAFTS
51) HEALTH
52) HEAL
53) JOY
54) ANGEL
55) PUZZLE
56) FORMULA
57) THROUGH
58) ASSIGNMENT
59) COG
60) KEY
61) LIFEDOOR
62) LISTEN
63) POWER
64) PATIENCE
65) LOOK
66) LAUGH
67) SERVE
68) SEEK
69) BRIDGES
70) TRUTH
71) OPEN
72) IS
73) IAM

Chapter 49

Yo Yos

Very short and sweet. The way I see it is that if we are *normal* we do what we are told. We are reeled out just so far, then we are reeled back where "they" want us. If we are *abnormal* we have opinions of our own and are considered *crazy*. You see people, either way we are all a bunch of yo-yos.

YO-YOS: *"My Journal Time"* – What do you think?

My Journal

My Journal

My Journal

Chapter 50

Zen

Zen is a word for meditation. You clear away everything and than have harmony. You live from moment to moment in awareness. You listen for messages and apply them to life. The gravel in a zen garden suggests flow of water (mind). It represents the flow of life and you focus on the gravel as you rake it. Add some rocks for security and stability (like a rock). Add cherry blossoms which stand for (the best-cherry). The bench and the quietness in a zen garden are for your (body). They suggest relaxation. The empty spaces in a zen garden represent the (soul). They suggest that you put the possibilities and your passions into the spaces.

ZEN: *"My Journal Time"* – Do you take Zen time? How? Think of an area around your home where you could put a Zen area or make a table top one.

My Journal

My Journal

My Journal

And Life Goes On
More Lessons

As I am completing the final stages to get this book to publication, I am once again reminded of the divine plan that always surprises us with the unexpected. I went back to Disney in April. I was rehired part time to add to my weekend marketing job income. On one of my off days, after only being back at Disney for three weeks, I had an accident. I fainted due to a fragrance allergy and due to the fall, I broke my hip. I caught myself saying, "What is this now?" As I know, there are no accidents. There is always a lesson to be learned. Was this a time for me to "Be"? And not "Do?"

Referring back to Quote ref. 88, "Pain makes man think." I knew I had to stop, look and listen. I thought to myself, I already did my five years at Disney from 2000- 2005, the agreement I made with myself. I need to move forward and have faith that God will give me my daily bread in His time. I also need to be true to myself. The fact that it was my hip that broke, this tells me that I need to move forward and be more balanced. This I learned from Book ref. 6.

I had a dream about bats during my recovery. The interpretation of this dream is that my current path is not compatible with my new growth and goals. My other dream about rice means success, prosperity and warm friendships. Disney is not the answer this time. I need to cut myself a new path because I have new growth and I have new goals. I need to leave my comfort zone and explore new horizons now. I need to be in the here and now, not the back then and there.

(Book ref. 32) "*Way of the Peaceful Warrior*" by Dan Millman "A warrior doesn't seek pain, but if pain comes, he uses it. Remember, the time is *now* and the place is *here*. The warrior is *here, now.*"

I need to have faith and realize that everything is given in the right time. As I write this, it is July 8, 2009. I open my Daily Word booklet for today. The heading for today is "Right Time."

(Daily Word ref. 39) "I take a God-moment and pray. As I do, I become peaceful and calm. Right now, in this moment, my attention is on what is true for me at all times: I am one with God."

For some reason I looked at the word for July 9. The word is Comfort. I flip the page again to July 10. The word is Faith.

(Daily Word ref. 40) "I am where I am meant to be to give and receive a blessing. I may share information that is just what someone needed to hear."

(Book ref. 0) "*The Language of Letting Go*" by Melody Beattie "Unfinished business doesn't go away. It keeps repeating itself until it gets our attention; until we feel it; deal with it, and heal."

(Book ref. 33) "*The Inner Path from Where You Are To Where You Want To Be.*" by Terry Cole-Whittaker "In the end we must be true to ourselves. All of us must be. If we are in a relationship we can no longer tolerate, we have to get out. If we are in a career field in which we do not experience joy and exultation, we must leave. If we are in an environment in which we feel we will suffocate and die, we must depart. If we are in any way unhappy, we must change the conditions causing our experience or we become slaves to those conditions. And we must do it come what may, or what may come could be a greater hell."

Conclusion

(Quote ref. 179) by George Bernard Shaw: *"This is the true joy of life: the being used up for a purpose recognized by yourself as a mighty one; being a force of nature instead of a feverish, selfish little clot of ailments and grievances, complaining that the world will not devote itself to making you happy."*

We are here to live in sweet success not toxic success.

(Book ref. 34) *"Toxic Success - How to stop striving and start thriving"* by Paul Pearsall "If toxic success is a state of constant distraction caused by pressure to do and have more, sweet success is attending fully to the now with confident contentment that enough is finally enough."

(Quote ref. 180) in this same book by John de Graff: *"Affluenza, painful, contagious, socially transmitted condition of overload, debt, anxiety, and waste resulting from the dogged pursuit of more."*

(Book ref. 14) *"In their own way"* by Thomas Armstrong – From the chapter A Worksheet Wasteland neglecting Talents And Abilities In Our Nations Schools.

(Quote ref. 181) by Jean Houston: *"How many thinkers and creative spirits are wasted, how much brain power goes down the drain because of our archaic, insular notions of brain and education? The numbers are undoubtedly horrendous."*

(Quote ref. 182) by Einstein: *"It is nothing short of a miracle that the modern methods of instruction have not yet entirely strangled the holy curiosity of inquiry."*

Always remember that your prayers are always answered, you are always given what you need.

(Quote ref. 183) by Alfred Lord Tennyson: *"More things are wrought by prayer than this world knows of."*

(Quote ref. 184) by Joan Borysenko: *"Rules of life: Show up, Pay attention, Tell the truth, Don't be upset at the results."*

(Quote ref. 185) by Joan Borysenko: *"Some tension is necessary for the soul to grow, we can put that tension to good use. We can look for every opportunity to give and receive love, to appreciate nature, to heal our wounds and the wounds of others, to forgive, and to serve."*

(Quote ref. 186) by Jonathan Livingston Seagull: *"Look with your understanding, find out what you already know, and you'll see the way to fly."*

(Quote ref. 187) by Buddha: *"A generous heart, kind speech, and a life of service and compassion are the things that renew humanity."*

(Quote ref. 188) by Robert Louis Stevenson: *"That man is a success who has lived well, laughed often and loved much; who has gained the respect of intelligent men and the love of children; who has filled his niche and accomplished his task; who leaves the world better than he found it whether by a perfect poem or a rescued soul; who never lacked appreciation of earth's beauty or failed to express it; who looked for the best in others and gave the best he had."*

(Daily Word ref. 41) "Like the disciples of Jesus, I act in partnership with the Christ. Through the Christ Spirit within me, I cooperate with those in my family, workplace, and community. The more willing I am to function in partnership with others, the more proficient I am at it."

(Daily Word ref. 42) "Focusing my mind on powerful, healing thoughts, I create a blessing of health for every one of the trillions of individual cells of my body."

(Bible ref. 39) Proverbs 4:7 " Wisdom is the principal thing; Therefore get wisdom – And in all your getting, get understanding."

(Lyrics ref. 48) *"Better get to livin"* - "Dolly, what's your secret? With all you do, your attitude – just seems to be so good. You better get to livin, givin. Don't forget to throw in a little forgivin – and lovin on the way – Cause all the healing has to start with you."

Peace be with you throughout your journey.

May you all have the wonderful life that you deserve.

Keep your life door open.

God bless.

Book References
Listed By Chapter Name

Preface:
Book Ref. 0 - The Language of Letting Go – Melody Beattie – Hazelden Foundation 1990

Introduction:
Book Ref.1 - Key to Yourself – Venice Bloodworth – Devorss & Company Marina del Ray, Ca 1952-1980

Spirituality:
Book Ref .2 - All the Joy You Can Stand – Debra Jackson Gandy – 3 Rives Press, Crown Publishing New York 2000

Formula/Assignment:
Book Ref. 3 - Unto the Hills – Billy Graham – W Publishing Group/ Thomas Nelson Nashville TN 1996

The Teen Years to 100 Plus:
Book Ref. 4 - Fire in the Belly – Sam Keen - Bantam Double Day Dell Pub. NY 1991

Experiences:
Book Ref. 5 - The Pilgrimage – Paulo Coelho – Harper Collins Publishers NY 1998

Book Ref. 6 - You Can Heal Your Life – Louise Hay – Hay House, Carlsbad, CA 1984

Book Ref. 7 -If Life Is a Game, These Are the Rules – Cherie Carter Scott PhD.Broadway Books, Bantam Double Day, Dell NY 1998

Book Ref. 8 - A Woman's Worth – Marianne Williamson – Ballantine Books, Random House NY 1993

Book Ref. 9 - Why Your Life Sucks – Alan H. Cohen – Jodere Group Inc. San Diego, CA 2002

Thoughts:
Book Ref. 10 - Flying Closer To the Flame – Charles Swindoll – Bantam, NY 1992
Book Ref. 11 - Wouldn't Take Nothing for My Journey Now – Maya Angelou – Random House, Canada 1993

Gratitude:
Book Ref. 12 - Simple Abundance – Daybook of Comfort And Joy – Sarah Ban Breathnach- Warner Books, NY 1995

Book Ref. 13 - The Artists Way – Julia Cameron – Penguin Putnam/ Tarcher, NY 1997

School:
Book Ref. 14 - In Their Own Way – Thomas Armstrong – Penguin Putnam Inc. NY 2000

Book Ref. 15 - Ants and The Grasshopper – Aesop's Fables – Scholastic Apple Classic – Retold by Ann McGovern, NY 1963

Assume:
Book Ref. 16 - The Four Agreements – Don Miguel Ruiz – Amber-Allen Publishing Co. San Rafael, CA 1997

Attachment:
Book Ref. 17 - Return to Love – Marianne Williamson – Harper Collins Pub. NY 1992

Body:
Book Ref. 18 - Sacred Pampering Principles – Debra Jackson Gandy – William Morrow & Company NY 1997

Book Ref. 19 - Creative Visualization – Shakti Gawain – Nataraj-Neward Library, Novato, 2002

Communication:
Book Ref.20 - Free To Be You and Me – Marlo Thomas – Free To Be Foundation Inc 1974

Compare/Competition:
Book Ref.21 - 12 Secrets of Highly Creative Women – Gail McMeekin – Conari Press, Berkeley, CA 2000

Dreams:
Book Ref. 22 -   The Element Encyclopedia OF 20,000 Dreams – Theresa Cheung – Barnes And Noble Inc. Harper 2006

Book Ref. 23 - Book of Dreams – Sylvia Browne – Nal Trade 2007

Health:
Book Ref.24 - Your Body Can Talk – Susan L. Levy – Hohm Press – Prescott, AZ 1996

Book Ref 25 - Walk In Balance – Sun Bear/Crysalis Mulligan/Peter Nufer-Wabun – Fireside-Simon Schuster NY 1989

Music and All the Arts:
Book Ref.26 - Joy Is My Compass – Alan Cohen – Hay House Inc., Carlsbad, CA 1990

Nature:
Book Ref.27 - Toxic Home and Office: Debra Lynn Dadd – Jeremy Tarchar/Putnam Pub.NY 1992

Book Ref.28 - Diet for a Poisoned Planet – David Steinman – Harmony Books – Crown Pub.NY 1990

Soul:
Book Ref. 29 - The Man Who Listens To Horses – Monty Roberts – Random House, Inc NY 1996

Understanding:
Book Ref. 30 - Tao the Ching – Lao Tzu – Shambhala Pub. Boston Mass. 1961

Vision Quest:
Book Ref. 31 - In the Meantime – Iyanla Vanzant – Simon Schuster NY 1998

Life Goes On:
Book Ref. 32 – Way of the Peaceful Warrior – Dan Millman – HJ Kramer Inc. New World Library, CA 1980

Book Ref. 33 - The Inner Path from Where You Are To Where You Want To Be - Terry Cole-Whittaker – Rawson Associates NY 1986

Conclusion:
Book Ref. 34 - Toxic Success - Paul Pearsall- Innerocean Pub. Hawaii 2002

Quote References

"*The Celestial Fortune Cookie*" by Andrea Valeria - Pub: Viking Studio Penguin Group NY 2000

"*Jupiter Signs*" by Madalyn Aslan Penguin Group NY 2004

"*Treasury of Women's Quotations*" by Carolyn Warner Prentice Hall Inc. 1992

Author's Notes: Other quotations were obtained from various unknown sources but, I did a considerable amount of research to give the authors their due credit.

Bible References

Inspirational Study Bible - New King James Version Max Lucado- General Edition- Word Publishing 1979 Thomas Nelson, Inc.

Definitions

"*The New American Webster Handy College Dictonary 3ʳᵈ Edition*" Prepared by: Philip D. Morehead – Editors: Albert & Loy Morehead 1995

Lyric References

Lyric references 1-48 were taken from various internet sites.

Daily Word References

Ref. 1- June 13, 2007

Ref 2 - June 26, 2005

Ref 3 - Sept.19, 2005

Ref 4- April 4, 2007

Ref 5- Aug. 5, 2006

Ref 6- Feb. 28, 2005

Ref 7- Oct. 31, 2006

Ref 8- March 1, 2005

Ref 9 - May 25, 2006

Ref 10- April 28, 2007

Ref 11- Aug. 20, 2006

Ref 12- April 19, 2006

Ref 13- March 30, 2005

Ref 14- April 9, 2005

Ref 15- Feb. 13, 2006

Ref 16- Jan. 29, 2007

Ref 17- March 17, 2007

Ref 18- Dec. 1, 2006

Ref 19- Feb 10, 2005

Ref 20- March 28, 2007

Ref 21- July 19, 2005

Ref 22- June 7, 2007

Ref 23- June 8, 2005

Ref 24- April 1, 2005

Ref 25- June 18, 2007

Ref 26- Dec. 9, 2005

Ref 27- Dec. 9, 2005

Ref 28- Jan. 24, 2006

Ref 29- Dec. 1, 2005

Ref 30- Aug. 21, 2006

Ref 31- Aug. 30, 2007 (World Peace Calendar)

Ref 32- April 6, 2005

Ref 33- July 28, 2005

Ref 34- June 26, 2005

Ref 35- March 13, 2005

Ref 36- March 2007 (Norman V. Olsson Poem)

Ref 37- Sept. 26, 2007

Ref 38- Oct. 10, 2007

Ref 39- July 8, 2009

Ref 40- July 10, 2009

Ref.41- Oct. 14, 2007

Ref.42- Oct. 15, 2007

About the Author

As I approached what I call the third stage of life, I sat down and had a long talk with myself. What would I like to do that I haven't done yet? My first answer, among many, was to write a book. It's simple philosophy and can be read by those 13 years old through 100+ years young. My qualifications to write about life are simple. I'm writing mostly from experiences. We are on this earth to share and since I have simplified my life in the last couple of years, I feel that now is the time to share my ideas. I invite you to use the information as you would like to and delete what is not useful to you, or maybe use it for the future. I am a seeker (Gnostic) rather than a believer (Dogma). I feel free, open and creative. Seeking alternatives brings unity by accepting what kind of relationship you want with Christ, rather than being told what to believe about Christ. Being Gnostic becomes a spiritual journey of finding self through many forms. I learned to become buddies with the Universe by being aware of all experiences, all thoughts and became grateful for everything, especially challenges and changes. Conformity is not a word in my vocabulary unless I'm using it to establish agreements and/or harmony. To comply to others wishes against my better judgment, or if something is hindering my growth or not letting me be true to myself, or if an outcome is not for the good of all those concerned, than that would be like selling my soul. To me, religion is only knowledge, accepting facts. It just sits there like a noun. Spirituality is wisdom and acts on what matters. It goes into action like a verb. Everything I wrote in this book is what I believe in now. If something does not work for me anymore in the future, then I know I can change that choice without retribution.